PROFESSIONALS EVERYWHERE HAVE HAILED DR. ARNOLD RINCOVER'S *THE PARENT-CHILD CONNECTION*

"*The Parent-Child Connection* fills a longstanding need — to make scientific findings on child development and child behavior problems available to parents. . . . Clearly written and rings true to our everyday experience with children. Parents will appreciate the practical explanations."
— Lynn E. McClannahan, Ph.D.,
Princeton Child Development Institute

"Exactly the kind of book that I think should be available to every parent. . . . Written at the right level with the right air of informality and directness. . . ."
— James M. Kauffman, Professor of Education,
University of Virginia

"There has long been a need for a parent-directed book on child rearing that bases its recommendations on proven behavioral principles. . . . *The Parent-Child Connection* [is] a most valuable contribution to the child-care literature for the lay public."
— Alan O. Ross, Ph.D.,
Department of Psychology,
State University of New York at Stony Brook

"Highly readable and technically sound . . . tells parents in practical, specific terms how to decide if there is or is not a problem . . . and, more to the point, what to do about it. . . . To date, *The Parent-Child Connection* is the only manual of its kind that I can recommend . . . without reservation."
— Cyril M. Franks, Ph.D., Distinguished University Professor,
Rutgers University

The Parent-Child Connection

Your Guide to Baby and Child Behavior in the First Six Years

Arnold Rincover, Ph.D.

POCKET BOOKS

New York   London   Toronto   Sydney   Tokyo

POCKET BOOKS, a division of Simon & Schuster Inc.
1230 Avenue of the Americas, New York, NY 10020

ISBN: 0-671-68164-8

First Pocket Books trade paperback printing January 1990

10 9 8 7 6 5 4 3 2 1

Originally published in Canada
by Random House of Canada Limited.

CONTENTS

PREFACE

BEING A PARENT CAN be an exhilarating, yet frightening experience. I have worked with hundreds of children and their families over the years, and I have two young ones of my own; so I have not only seen and tried to help many concerned parents, but I have been one. I have watched my son bang his head on the crib and wondered, with my heart in my mouth, if there was something wrong with him. I have watched my children grow, and found myself asking the same questions virtually every parent has asked of me: "Is my child normal?"; "Will he grow out of it?"; "What should I do?" None of us has been trained on how to be a good parent, so it is quite natural and normal to ask such questions. The purpose of this book is to answer those questions.

This guide is designed for all parents with young (newborn-to six-year-old) children. In general, most parents seem to fall into one of three groups. First, some parents think there is a problem, but really there is not, since "normal" child development does include some periods of bizarre (and upsetting) activities, such as self-injury, noncompliance, tantrums, sleeplessness, and ritualistic behavior. This is by far the largest group of parents. It will be comforting, we hope, for these parents to know that the suspect behavior is actually quite normal and their child will probably grow out of it. A second group of parents may be concerned about real, though limited, behavioral excesses or deficits of their child: one family is upset because their child isn't eating;

another is concerned their child isn't speaking yet; a third is alarmed at how aggressive, oppositional, or bratty their child is. We will describe for these parents how to tell when it is a problem and what can be done about it. A third group of parents is faced with more severe problems, such as the possiblity of autism or retardation, and we will describe the assessment, treatment, and professional resources available to those parents. Whether or not the problem is real, or the behavior severe, it is your child, and the problem may well be all-consuming until you get some answers. We all wonder at times if there is something wrong with our baby, and we need to know how and where to find the answers.

The greatest source of frustration for me over the years has been the often preventable and unnecessary emotional stress in parents. By the time I see them, the problem is often much worse, and could have been treated much more easily and effectively if dealt with sooner. There are countless tales of psychologists, pediatricians, psychiatrists, child-development and assessment clinics saying that the two-year-old will probably "grow out of it," and then a short year or two later a parent is faced with the grim diagnosis of emotional, social, or intellectual disorders. Many parents also get several opinions, and are shocked to find they all differ. Some parents are told they simply have to "live with it," when the truth is they don't, and it is often a fairly simple problem to deal with. While there are many excellent books telling us what normal child development looks like, such as the classic *Baby & Child Care* by Dr. Benjamin Spock, there are none showing us how to tell when there is a problem, and what to do about it. There is no comprehensive, objective source to which I can refer parents in dealing with questions about their child's behavior. This book, then, is intended as a "companion to Dr. Spock," to show specifically when there is and is not a problem, why a child is behaving that way, and what a *parent* can do about it.

It is hoped that this Guide will be helpful to all new parents, yet it is important to clarify both its scope and its limitations at the outset. First, the majority of this book will be based upon research. No descriptions of treatment, principles, or behavior are based upon opinions of mine, or anyone else's; they are objective descriptions based upon reliable research, systematic evaluation, and known principles of child development. This is because opinions come cheap (anyone can have one) and are not to be confused with fact; an opinion is an opinion *because* its author does not have sufficient facts or data to back it up. When opinions are expressed here, and there are some in certain portions of the book, the reader should recognize that these are based only on my own recollections, experiences, and thoughts, subject to all the biases and vagaries my own history and experience bring to bear.

In terms of content, the book will cover most of the social, psychological, and intellectual concerns parents have about their children in the first six years of life. These will include: aggression, crying, tantrums, hyperactivity, language, fears and phobias, oppositional behavior, social behavior, attachment, head-banging and self-injury, ritualistic and compulsive behavior, sleeping and feeding problems, and others. In each case, we will describe what the behavior looks like, when it is and is not a problem, and what a parent can do about it. The book will not, however, cover physical, genetic, or known neurological handicaps, because that would involve going beyond my own areas of expertise and clinical experience. Neither will it cover problems specific to older children, such as truancy and stealing, even though some of the same parenting principles apply.

This book will also deal specifically with the anxieties and frustrations of parents. We will try to explain what "abnormal" means, and whether abnormal behavior is permanent or temporary. We will try to describe some concerns of parents that are really nothing to worry about. We will explain "assessment," "diagnosis," and "prognosis" in layman's terms; consider when you need to get one or the other; and describe their limitations, uses, and misuses. We will discuss some hard questions that parents and families may face when they are "at their wits' end": frustration, guilt, and stresses on the marriage and other family members. We will describe the functions and roles of different kinds of professionals, and some characteristics to look for and avoid in selecting professionals and programs. We will also review the most common questions and mistakes of parents: looking for a "magic pill"; searching out an "optimistic" assessment; denying the problem; and trying to find a balanced family/social life. It is hoped that by demystifying our profession, listening to the questions of other parents who have been in similar situations, and learning from the successes and failures of various coping strategies, that we can help to minimize the frustration and stress to parents and siblings.

There is one final caveat about the scope and limitations of this book. Every child is different. In fact, even two children who engage in the same behavior may have entirely different causes and treatments. It is therefore impossible to describe every conceivable, effective program for each possible nuance of each problem behavior. Consequently, this book cannot and should not replace professional supervision and assistance. Rather, this book will describe principles that have been shown to have some generality for all children, and illustrative programs and cases will be given. Parents should not feel the least bit hesitant to seek some advice or help, from a professional, if they feel unable to handle the problem. At the very least, the supervision will confirm that what you are planning for your child is in fact best; or perhaps someone with more experience will have some insights that will help to devise a better program for your particular child.

This then is a book for parents who are concerned about their child's behavior. It will explain why children act the way they do; it will describe, specifically, things that are cause for concern, and things that are not; it will describe strategies for handling the situation when necessary; and it will illustrate when parents are part of the problem and when they are part of the solution.

ACKNOWLEDGMENT

There are many people to thank for their contributions to this book. The Colbert Agency and Ed Carson of Random House both guided me with constructive (yet gentle) advice, and generally held my hand throughout this new adventure. My wife, Lawanna, played more roles than I can possibly describe — from editor to teacher to friend; without her, there simply would have been no book. To my parents and my children, I dedicate this book, for it is they who taught me about child-rearing from both sides of the fence — they taught me the heart and soul of it, which cannot be found in any research journal. Finally, there were many, many people who helped me with the text, from interpreting my scribbling into readable text, to commenting on the sum and substance of the book. To all these people, I am deeply grateful.

The
Parent-Child
Connection

1

PARENTAL QUESTIONS AND CONCERNS

THERE ARE LITTLE THINGS parents worry about, and there are big things parents worry about. I worried about them all. Do other parents play with their kids more than I do? How could I be so low as to use the TV as a baby sitter while I catch my breath? Is he smart? Shouldn't I be teaching her more? Do I spend enough time with them? Shouldn't she be talking by now? And on, and on, and on . . . .

In most cases, our concern will turn out to be brief, unnecessary, and sometimes even silly. I used to worry that neighbors and friends might see me outside with a He-Man mask, sword, and Mickey Mouse ears, playing with imaginary friends or planning our attack on the forces of evil. You know what? All the neighbors thought I was a great daddy *because* I did this. All I had to do was show up with Mickey Mouse ears once a week, and I was everyone's ideal daddy. (It is important , however, to always have a child with you when you do this – anybody's child will do.)

Parents have been bringing up children for hundreds and hundreds of years – parents with much less knowledge than we have. As a result, evolution has allowed children to withstand great variability in child-rearing practices. For centuries, kids have withstood our ignorance and mistakes; they are survivors.

At the same time, we want our children to do more than "survive." We want them to be bright, moral, socially skilled, and emotionally healthy. That's why parents worry. If we see our child doing something unusual or inappropriate, we'll worry that, maybe, this time, the child won't grow out of it and he won't be emotionally sound, socially appropriate, moral, or bright. So parents will continue to have the same concerns, the same questions, for generations to come – it is part and parcel of being a parent.

For each behavior in question, there is a point or time when we can either breathe a sigh of relief, knowing that it was not a problem after all, or else know that it is a problem that needs to be dealt with. This book will describe those points – when we can know that it is or is not a problem – and discuss what one can do if the problem behavior doesn't go away on time.

Do other children do this?

This question of course arises most often when your child does something sneaky, mean, aggressive, oppositional, or perhaps something just unusual and scary to you, like stuttering, banging his head against the wall, not eating, or repetitively spinning in circles. Virtually all children do all of these things at some time. Different children may do them in different ways: my son's aggressive episodes ranged from scratching my face to six-foot kamikaze dives at an unattentive daddy; one little girl was very adept at throwing toys, fruit, and dishes; another boy got to use the swing by first knocking other children off it. The point is that all children will be aggressive at some time, though it may take different forms. In a similar fashion, most children will at times be mean, oppositional, noncompliant, lie, hit, steal, pull your hair, stick their finger up your nose or down your throat. But this is no cause for alarm. These problems are in fact as normal and common as having children.

While it is true that virtually all children will do these things, what is of concern is *how long they continue to do them*. I was not (too) alarmed when my two-year-old son scratched my face, but I would have been if he was still doing it six months later; it did not worry me (too much) that my daughter was stuttering when she was three, but if she had continued stuttering at five it would have been a problem; I did not worry (too much) when my son first pushed another child, poured milk in the goldfish bowl, banged his head against the wall, or threw a toy at his mother, but I would have been very worried if these things had continued for very long.

Of course, I was not happy to see any of this, but the point is that I only had to worry about that moment, not whether he was and would forever be selfish, a bully, a spoiled brat, or have speech problems. It is that concern for the future, what it will lead to, that causes the greatest anxiety in most parents.

There is nothing we can do about the initial appearance of such behaviors – all children will try them – but *how we react to each* when it first appears will have a major effect on whether or not it continues. There is something we can do to prevent it from continuing too long. What is "too long," and how we might handle it, is discussed individually for each behavior in Part 4.

Why is he acting like this?

It is important to understand *why* children do these things. It is important because the reason will dictate to a large extent what we can do about it, and how we can insure that the exasperating or scary behavior doesn't last too long.

Young children don't have a very rich verbal repertoire, so the only way for them to really communicate is by *doing* something. Much of what a child does, good or bad, is a form of communication; he's telling you something. When a three-month-old baby cries, she is usually "telling you" that she is hungry, wet, tired, afraid, hurt, or in an uncomfortable position; when a three-month-old baby cries, I jump. By the time a child is a year old, the behavioral "vocabulary" has expanded. For example, there are different kinds of crying. Crying can mean "I want some attention," "I want a toy to play with," "I want to see over here," "I don't want to go to bed," "I don't want a bottle," as well as the old standbys, "I'm hurt (cold, tired, etc.)"; when this child cries, I don't jump as high or as often (see Part 4, Crying). By the time that child is three or four, his behavioral vocabulary is a lot more elaborate. A tantrum can mean that she wants to do it *now*, not soon; he wants to play with *that* toy, not this one; she wants to wear *these* shoes (shirt, dress), not those shoes; or she wants to eat spaghetti, not meat and potatoes. When this child laughs, it means he likes it; when he throws it aside, he's telling you he doesn't like it anymore. Similarly, when he pulls your arm, it may mean he wants to be held, or to play; when he bites your arm, it may mean he doesn't want to play at *that*, or perhaps you're ignoring him.

His play, his wants, his fantasies, are all developing rapidly, and his speech can't keep up; so, how else can he express himself but by behaving? He has no alternative. The three- to four-year-old child is becoming more and more discriminating (i.e. pickier) and his behavioral repertoire is expanding to match (express) it. He is learning which behavior will get your attention, which tell you that something is wrong, and which tell you something is right.

The point is, we must listen to what the child does, notice why he's doing it, before we can understand and handle the behavior in question.

Will my child grow out of it?

There are some things that children often do grow out of, and it can be comforting to know that if we can just get over the hump, it will be all right. Most children stutter, bang their heads, don't like to sleep alone, and seem at times to be hyperactive. But the very large majority of kids do grow out of these things, without any special effort on our part.

There are some things, however, that children do not always "grow out of." Fears, tantrums, aggression, and so on (see Part 4) can persist or worsen. And it is hard to predict which behaviors will disappear, and which will get worse. What is important, then, is to monitor the behavior, keep an eye on it, so you can tell if it is growing or abating. If tantrums continue too long, seem to increase, get more intense, become more frequent, then it is time to do something about it; if, on the other hand, they seem to decrease, then you need not worry.

In short, the *child* will "tell" you if he will grow out of it; the problem is not that the behavior occurs, but whether or not it persists, and it is difficult ahead of time to know which behavior will persist and which will disappear naturally.

Is there something I can do?

Most of the time, there is. What one can do will depend on *why* the child is behaving that way. We will describe here a number of reasons (motivations) for different behaviors, to show how the knowledge of motivation will determine how to handle the behavior.

Sometimes children behave inappropriately in an attempt *to get something they want*. At one time, my son would only eat Cheerios, would only wear one favorite (He-Man) T-shirt, and would "insist" on a new toy if he came within 8,000 miles of a toy store, saw a picture of toys or a toy store, saw a new toy at a friend's house, dreamt of a new toy, or just felt like a "surprise." And he would whine, pout, yell at me, or refuse to move (a favorite action of his), if he didn't get his way, or didn't get his way quickly enough. At first, trying to be the perfect, loving parents, who wanted our child to have rights and choices and some control over his life, we washed that shirt every night, took Cheerios camping and to the beach, and figured all these toys were "enriching" and "stimulating" (i.e. healthy) for him. Oh, what fools we were! On a day that we ran out of Cheerios, hadn't had time to wash his T-shirt, or didn't have money for the toy, he went bananas. The "insistence," which was a mild tantrum to begin with, flourished into a full-blown, foot-stomping, crying, dive-on-the-floor, wailing, floor-beating, refrigerator-door-slamming doozy. The very first time we saw this, we swore than *no* tantrum, mild or severe, would ever again "work" to get his way. From then on, he got to wear his favorite shirt only when we did (all) the wash and when it was dirty it just lay in the hamper until we did (all) the wash. We did try to still give him some choice – "Do you want to wear this shirt or that shirt?" – but neither of them was the (He-Man) shirt, and one of these two went on, and quickly, tantrum or not. The tantrums didn't work anymore, and they gradually subsided and virtually disappeared. I've read dozens of studies on this, but for some reason I was still surprised it actually worked with *my* child. It did, and relatively quickly.

Sometimes a child behaves inappropriately in order to *avoid* something, rather than to get something. Most children hate to go to bed, don't like medicine, don't like to "tidy up" after carefully arranging (pouring) all their toys on the living-room floor. If a tantrum serves to delay going to bed ("OK, you can stay up for just a little while."), the tantrum will only get worse next time you try putting him to bed . . . and worse . . . and worse. In this case, where the tantrum is to avoid something, the strategy is different: we must teach the child that a tantrum will not serve to avoid anything. Consequently, we follow through: when it's time to go to bed, even if he throws a tantrum to avoid it, he goes to bed, period. When it's time to go to bed, and *before* a tantrum has occurred, we may give the child a choice: "Do you want to go to bed now or in five minutes?" ("Five minutes.") "OK, then, it'll be time to go to bed at 9:25." Then he goes to bed at 9:25, come hell or high water. If he throws a tantrum, we explain (once) that we asked and *he* said 9:25, but any explanation occurs as we're heading up to bed – it does not delay it. Either way, we insure that the tantrum does not serve to prevent, avoid, or delay things. Adding a choice, by the way, seemed in many cases to help prevent or eliminate the tantrums, as children very often were appeased by (or appreciated) having a choice. But the choice must be given *before* a tantrum occurs (i.e. when I first decide that it's bedtime); if instead it follows a tantrum, it will give the tantrums a function (i.e. the tantrum would *serve* to get him a choice, and to delay bedtime for five minutes), and this would increase the child's use of tantrums.

Sometimes, children do worrisome things *because they are afraid*. This requires yet a different strategy. Let's suppose, for example, that a child has trouble sleeping. If the problem is that he plays with toys in bed until midnight, then it probably isn't fear that is keeping him up, and we should remove some of the toys (during the day). If on the other hand, he lies there, eyes as big as saucers, checking under the bed, saying he's afraid, or if he wakes up in the night sweating, crying, talking about monsters, then we go in and comfort him, hold him, read a (happy) story, talk to him. In addition, we check to see what toys, TV shows, games, preschool activities occurred that day, to see if they included goblins, snakes, or monsters; we arrange for them not to occur for a while. We ask the child what he is afraid of (i.e. "there's a monster under the bed"), show him that there's nothing under the bed, tell him we're here, put his "magic crystal" next to him that scares away dragons, goblins, and monsters with it's mystical super-powers, tell him his favorite hero will stay here and watch over him (get a doll or puppet of his hero), and so on. In short, when the worrisome behavior is related to fear, we try to remove objects or activities during the day that may conjure up the fears, comfort him through the anxious moments, and give him some control (by using the magic crystal, the super-hero in bed with him, lights on, etc.) over the feared object.

Sometimes, children do inappropriate things *just to satisfy their own curiosity*. They may taste your coffee, suck on a cigarette butt, or pick things up off the floor or out of the cupboard. Of more concern is that they might *like* something inappropriate – the texture or taste of a cigarette butt, rocks, or colorful medicine capsules. In such cases, we may hide them if we can, say: "NO, it might make you sick," or, perhaps best of all, soak the item in vinegar, Tabasco, or any other taste the child does not like, so that she will *not* like the object. Again, by figuring out *why* the child is doing it (i.e. taste), we can arrange it so that he doesn't get that good taste from it.

Sometimes, children act inappropriately *because they don't know the appropriate way to act*. Young children will often echo what you say, or part of what you say, when they don't understand it; this is called "Echolalia." (One parent asked his four-year-old whether he would like to vacation in Hawaii or the Caribbean. The child had no idea what daddy was asking, so he echoed the last word, "Caribbean." The father would have saved a lot of money by asking the child if he wanted to go to the Caribbean or the corner park.) Similarly, children may throw a tantrum for things because they don't know an appropriate way to get what they want. They may do "mean" things to animals or other, smaller children because they don't know how to interact with them in an enjoyable way. They can get hyperactive, frustrated, or aggressive if something is too hard, or not well understood. In such situations, we will teach them appropriate (but simple) ways to interact, or to get what they want; we'll make sure to explain things so they understand us; and we'll just stop saying or asking things that they can't understand.

Unquestionably, the most common reason (motivation) for inappropriate behavior is simply *to get attention*. From about six months to five years of age, a child's major source of pleasure in this world is attention from his parents. It's a special time – they're not into a peer group, classes, a counterculture, or money . . . yet. It is truly amazing how much we can teach our children, how dramatically we can influence them, with praise and attention. In fact, it is so powerful that children will go to great lengths to get it. They will try anything and everything, from playfully sticking a finger in your ear to get a reaction, to climbing on your back or head, to stabbing you with a (toy) sword. They will throw dolls at you, push you off the sofa, bite your arm, and put scotch tape on your glasses, if you dare to be preoccupied. They'll pull your hair, beg, yell, pinch, and hit you with a pillow, if you don't tune in fast enough. If we know it's for attention, we pick (attend, play, react to) the behavior that we want to "work" (i.e. asking, climbing on your lap, pulling your hand), *and* we do not attend or play when we are hit, yelled at, cried at, or stabbed. In addition, if the child is old enough, we can *tell* him proper ways to get our attention (say "Daddy," ask nicely, tap my arm, and various gestures). Then, the child will learn appropriate ways to get attention, and inappropriate behavior will no longer work.

There are many more reasons that children engage in inappropriate behavior, and we'll talk about them as we progress through the individual behaviors in Part 4. The above examples are common ones, and serve to illustrate how very important it is to know *why* a child is doing something.

To illustrate the danger of not knowing the motivation for a child's behavior, let's think through what could happen.

Let's say a child starts screaming, crying, throwing toys, jumping up and down – your normal, warlike tantrum. You may go over to comfort him, or you may send him to his room, say "Stop that," ignore him, or ask what's wrong. But what if he had been told to "tidy up," and he didn't want to? All of these reactions would get him out of tidying up. These procedures, then, would actually strengthen the problem behaviour. What if it's for attention? Many of these reactions do give him attention for throwing tantrums, and thereby strengthen and reinforce the behavior. Alternatively, what if another child had hit him? None of these reactions address the problem, most are unjust and unfair, and, worst of all, most teach the child that you are not there when he needs you.

Love is *not* enough, though it does go a long way. We must be aware of what we are teaching our children. And if we act unknowingly, then we will at times be teaching or strengthening the very (inappropriate) behavior that we are scared of, accidental and unintended though it may be.

What is "normal" and "abnormal" behavior?

It's a tough question. It's tough because the difference between normal behavior and abnormal behavior is usually a matter of degree, not form.

Very few behaviors are themselves inherently good or bad, normal or abnormal. They become abnormal if they occur in the wrong place, if they last too long, if they occur too frequently (or infrequently), or if they're too intense or excessive for the situation. Surely there's nothing wrong with smiling. Yet if a child smiles when he sees a friend hurt, we are going to worry; if the child never smiles, we are going to worry; if the child laughs hysterically for three hours at a silly face, and she does this too often, parents will worry and others will avoid her at all costs. The point is that virtually any action – singing, playing, being afraid, smiling, hugging, or fighting – can be appropriate or inappropriate, normal or abnormal, depending upon the context in which it occurs, the degree to which it occurs, and its intensity or frequency.

A behavior will also become abnormal if it interferes with routine daily activities. All children (and adults) have fears, moods, fights, and rituals. They (and we) are all at times hyper-active, and act very differently with different people. When does this become a split personality, a phobia, hyperactivity, a com-pulsion, a mood (emotional) disorder? If it interferes with nor-mal, daily activities, we may have a problem: if the high activity level is fairly constant, and it prevents him from participating in group activities, storybook reading, and sleeping at night; if a fear of dirt prevents a child from going outdoors, or causes him to be washing all the time, and this in turn interferes with other activities; if moods and emotions change radically at random and unpredictable times, rather than at proper and predictable times; and if fighting is inappropriate and common enough to in-terfere regularly with preschool activities, or playing with other children. In general, if any behavior has the effect of interfering substantially with normal daily activities, the behavior must be dealt with, by the parents or with professional assistance.

Some behaviors are abnormal in the sense that they simply bother you a lot. A child may not share his toys, he may not be toilet-trained, he may play violent games, or be a bit too opposi-tional for you (even if other kids are worse). One can be dissatis-fied about such things, even when that state of affairs is not at all uncommon in other children or families. In short, *parents often decide for themselves* what is abnormal, excessive, or unacceptable. It is abnormal with respect to their own experiences or stan-dards, rather than to some communal or external norms. (At the same time, parents should read Part 2, carefully, and consider when the problem is the child's behavior and when the problem lies with the parents and their expectations.)

If "abnormal" behavior is viewed in this way – as behavior out of context, excessive, interfering, or unduly upsetting – much of the stigma and mystery disappears. First, this definition implies that it is behavior patterns that are abnormal, not children. Second, behavior is modifiable, not immutable; therefore, ab-normal behavior is not necessarily permanent. Third, any stigma from "needing help" or "needing a special program" should be removed, since it is normal for children to have abnormal be-havior – we all will feel extremely upset about some of the things our children do.

Early intervention

It is very important to catch a problem early. It is important for at least two reasons. First, in general, the longer a behavior problem lasts, the worse it gets. Second, the early years, to the age of five or six, appear to contain "critical periods" or sensitive times for learning certain things; some things that are very difficult to teach children over five are much easier to teach to three- and four-year-olds. Let's take these one at a time.

The longer a behavior problem lasts, *the more elaborate it becomes*; it acquires more functions and uses, and it becomes more severe and intense. Furthermore, the stronger it is and the more uses it has, the harder it will be to eliminate. For example, if a two- or three-year-old has these devilish tantrums to get attention, the strategy can be fairly straightforward – give lots of attention when he is not throwing a tantrum, and no attention when he is (elaborations on this are given in Part 4). If, however, these tantrums are allowed to continue for a few years, they will eventually be "used" for a whole host of reasons – to get a cookie, a toy, the chair you're sitting in; to go outside, have a party, or watch TV; to go this way when you have to go that way, do this when you have to do that; to get out of cleaning up, taking a bath, taking medicine, moving from the sofa, going to somebody's house; and so on. Then, it becomes much, much more difficult to deal with. Furthermore, the fact that tantrums have lasted two years means that they have served a purpose for a long, long time – they're well established and more resistant to treatment. So, *any* treatment will take longer, and will be more traumatic and emotional (for parents as well as the child).

In addition, the behavior will *generalize or transfer* more – to new settings, situations, and people – the longer the behavior lasts. That is, the behavior starts to "spread" all over the place. A child who pushes, hits, or yells at mommy to get his way, may after a year or two be found to do the same to other children, teachers, siblings, strangers, and friends.

Third, the longer an inappropriate behavior lasts, the more the child will *develop other, similar inappropriate behaviors*. What starts out as an inappropriate behavior turns into a general style (i.e.

aggression) of interacting. What may start out as pushing, can easily develop into a broad arsenal of kicking, hitting, pinching, fighting, yelling, rock throwing, and so on.

Finally, the longer it lasts, the more chance there is of negative *side-effects*. A child who is overly aggressive may, because of the aggression, be expelled from preschool, swimming class, children's camp; he may become less attractive to family, siblings, and other children; and he may not learn other, appropriate ways to negotiate, compromise, share, or otherwise solve his problems. The result can be a loss of recreational opportunities and skills, less bonding between the child and his family, poorer social skills (sincerity, friendship, compassion, co-operation, sharing), and possibly even depression and isolation. To take another example, the three-year-old thinks nothing of his stuttering. Yet, if he is still stuttering at five or six, he may begin to feel "different" than his friends, shyer about going to a birthday party or a friend's house, afraid to say anything in public. This child may become insular, aloof, sad and depressed, feign illness to get out of going to public places, and become extremely distressed and anxious when public places cannot be avoided.

Clearly, it is very important to catch the behavior early, to prevent these potentially heartbreaking side-effects, and to minimize the strength or growth of the behavior.

As we mentioned, there is yet another reason for tackling problems as early as possible – "critical periods" or sensitive times for learning certain things seem to come in the first five to six years.

Given the same treatment procedures, seven- to ten-year-old children have a much more difficult time learning certain basic social skills than do younger two- to four-year-old children. For example, if a child does not respond to (enjoy) praise, hugs, attention, or the closeness of other people, these can be very difficult to establish in older children – yet much simpler in younger children.

It has also been found that newly learned behaviors will often generalize all over the place in young children, yet may not in older children. For example, if we can teach a child how to talk without stuttering, younger children may quickly adopt these new (fluency) skills everywhere, while the adolescent may only be able to speak fluently at home, or in the presence of the helper or parent. More help will often be needed for the older child, in each of a variety of situations, to get this fluency to appear everywhere.

The (young) child who generalizes, of course, has a tremendous advantage: if a child learns a new word ("Hi"), and says "Hi" to grandma, friends, and neighbors, these people will react, elaborate on it, model other new social and verbal skills ("Well I'm fine, thank you, and how are you?"; "All right, gimme five"; "My name's Ralph, what's your name?"; "Are you my friend? Let's shake on it."), and at the same time the child will naturally get more attention, hugs, caresses, and longer and more enjoyable social engagements.

Language also appears much easier to learn at an early age (note how young children so easily pick up a second language, while smarter, but older, adults spend years struggling with vocabulary and verb tenses, and still end up talking with "an accent"). While young children often "learn to learn," and speech difficulties can be made up rapidly, older children with speech problems often learn much more slowly and laboriously.

In general, then, we have two major reasons to intervene early. First, we must prevent *a problem behavior* from gaining strength, from expanding into a larger arsenal, and from turning into a general style of interaction. Second, many *appropriate behaviors* are more easily taught at an early age.

A final, important note: these two advantages of early intervention complement each other quite nicely because *it is always better to replace an inappropriate behavior with an appropriate behavior, rather than to just eliminate the inappropriate behavior.* If we remember that inappropriate behavior is communication, then how will the child continue to "tell" you things if you're eliminating some of his behavior? I'd be afraid to think of what the child might come up with next (very possibly something more extreme and more inappropriate), and we'd be leaving it to chance. Instead, we can show him, teach him, an appropriate way to communicate what he wants. If a child throws banana peels, spits grape seeds, or pours cereal on the floor, we don't just tell him not to do that, we teach (show/tell) him the right way to handle it (perhaps to put it in the trash); if he grabs a toy out of another child's hands, we don't just reprimand him and explain why not, we show him how to ask nicely, how to offer his toy in exchange, how to ask for a turn in a few minutes. In this way, the child is not just learning what not to do, but we are also teaching him a new, appropriate way to behave, so he *does* get what he wants. And we are actually quite fortunate because, as we've seen, teaching the new (appropriate) behavior *and* eliminating the problem behavior are both much easier to do if we catch the problem early.

Common concerns of parents

Many parents come to a psychologist seeking reassurance that there is no real problem. Most of the time, we can give that assurance; as we've noted earlier, many parental anxieties are in truth unfounded. Sometimes, however, there are problems that need to be handled. Acknowledging, facing, and tackling such problems, whether they be minor or major, physical or behavioral, can be a holy trauma for a parent. My son broke his leg at the age of three, while jumping on a bobo doll. We took him to the emergency room, where he was put in traction (in the hospital) for three weeks, then in a cast for eight more weeks. I was *sure* that we had the worst doctor, nurses, x-ray technician, and cast-maker; I got 800 other opinions. I was sure they weren't watching him enough, the splint and cast weren't set quite right, and they had received their diplomas from a mail-order course. We were grief-stricken to hear that one leg might be a quarter-inch shorter that the other – what would happen to his love of sports, his physical development, his self-image, his confidence? I vacillated unmercifully between rage, anxiety, concern, self-pity; I was contemplating my zillion-dollar lawsuit against the doctors, the hospital, the city, and the bobo doll . The point is, when your child has a problem – any kind of problem, whether it be physical, behavioral, emotional, or social – it can be awfully hard to face, or to be rational, at least for a while. And I see this same sort of difficulty, the same questions and concerns, in parents who bring their children to me.

Most parents, who have a real, persistent problem concerning their child's behavior, want some help quickly. They are more familiar with medical problems and treatments, so they want a prescription, *a magic pill* that works quickly ("take two of these, three times a day, and we'll *kill* the dreaded behavior"). When it's not possible to do something like that – that fast – they get discouraged. It's understandable, though. Parents want to hear that their child is basically fine; it's just a little thing; there's nothing to worry about. But that would be *denying the problem*. There is no infection; there is no virus; and usually (not always) pills won't help. We have to plan a program, and the parents often have to help carry it out.

This is not what many parents want to hear, so they may seek another opinion, and another, and another, searching for a quick cure, one that allows them to preserve the initial view (hope) that it's really nothing. Seeking a second opinion is, of course, not only OK, but highly recommended. But we seek a second opinion in order to find out if a second person will arrive at the same conclusions as the first; if so, we then have more confidence the first was right, and we can act on it. The problem arises when a parent seeks another opinion *because* the second opinion agreed with the first (i.e. the parents didn't like the first), and they continue seeking opinions in the hope of finding one that does *not* agree with the first. So, after *getting a tenth opinion*, they'll either face the facts, or waste precious time (see "Early intervention," above) with a professional who told them what they wanted to hear.

When, finally, faced with the realization that we've got some work to do here, parents may then go *looking for an optimist*. It's bad enough that there is a problem that needs some special attention, but at least they're going to find someone who will say, in his best bedside manner, that "everything's going to be all right." I don't care if you're seeing a lawyer, a doctor, a tax advisor, a psychologist, or a financial planner, we all wait with bated breath until we hear those magic words, "Everything's going to be all right."

Usually, everything will be all right, if we face the situation. It does not usually require an elaborate, extensive, or time-consuming plan; it just requires a parent to understand that there are no magic or quick cures, and that we can take care of it if we make a few changes in how we interact with the child (i.e. react to the behavior).

In other families, parents do just the opposite. They may accept anything the first psychologist says. Whoever they see is a *"messiah,"* all-knowing, all-wise, all-caring, all-worldly. When faced with such a person, we may lose our critical eye (i.e. does this program really make sense for our child? Is it practical?). Moreover, we may attribute to this professional powers and wisdom to solve any other problems we have ("you know . . . my husband doesn't know how to handle a child, what should I do?"; "The problem is my wife's a nagger; can you cure her, too?"; "I've got these weird dreams. . . ."). We tend to attribute to people who are truly expert in one area a similar wisdom and knowledge in many other, unrelated areas (that they actually may know little about). This is why a famous athlete or movie star is employed on TV to tell us about the wonders of certain coffee machines, soda pops, and the benefits of retractable razors. This is why famous scientists are asked to speak on politics, war, and unemployment – if they're that smart in physics, then they must be smart in everything they speak about. No one has this much knowledge or wisdom (certainly not psychologists); we each have to specialize in certain areas to become truly expert at it. Even different expert psychologists will conclude and suggest different things, so it is crucial never to accept such opinions without scrutiny or consideration. (See the Epilogue for some things to consider in separating good from not-so-good psychologists.)

Some parents get extreme in yet another direction. They not only face the problem and deal with it, they do little else. The problem is blown way out of proportion. They are consumed by the child, the treatment, the program; the rest of the family, the rest of life, gets pretty short shrift. In such cases, we must help the person *look for a balanced family life*: social events are important, other family members need some tending and attention, and we all need to have some fun. In addition, one needs to put it in perspective, so the problem does not cast a shadow over the child and his/her other behaviors. It does no good to be consumed by it, and make everyone's life miserable in the process, unintentional though it may be.

Sometimes, our concern will be more about us as parents, rather than the child's behavior. Most of us are unnerved at how many times we really just *don't know what to do*. No one ever taught us how to be a parent, how to bring up a child; "I couldn't even keep my goldfish alive, how am I going to care for a child?" Yet there are minutes, even days, during the child-rearing years when our confidence grows, we feel able, our child is doing something great (maybe even something we taught him – a golden, inflating moment). Then, there are those other days . . . when we are sure we have no right to be a parent; we wonder how God could let such a schlepp become a parent, and so easily, with no application forms or interviews. (What would we have put on a résumé, under experience – "My plants lasted a week, my goldfish two"? "We had a dog and he lived"?) We really don't come into the job with very impressive credentials, do we?

The short answer to this is that nature will carry us a long way, and knowledge will take us the rest. Some parenting skills come naturally, some we learn from the way in which we were brought up, and some we learn from asking, talking to people, and reading. A lot of it comes from on-the-job training, /i.e. trial and error. We may not do it systematically, or attack it like a classroom course, but we do get it, incidentally, a bit here and a bit there. Often, this will suffice; sometimes, however, there will still be situations where we don't know what to do. Hopefully, this book will help to fill in whatever gaps the reader may have.

Another concern parents often have about themselves has to do with those times, in every parent's life, when it all just seems too much. At such times, we're sure to feel everyone else isn't doing their share (see Part 2). We will have some *"evil thoughts,"* about our kids, our spouse, and anyone else foolish enough to walk through the door. "My kid is really rotten"; "My daughter is spoiled"; "Sometimes I hate them"; *"Sometimes I want to scream/strangle them."* This can, in fact, reflect just how much you care, how hard you're trying, and what a tough job it really is. We all need a break at times. In fact, each of the family members will go through this, so it's wise to help and understand each other at such times – it will be returned in kind.

A problem arises, however, when this happens too often. If it gets to the point where you need to get away quite often, or are constantly dissatisfied with the kids and family, or if you find your "evil" thoughts outweigh your good thoughts, then something very fundamental is wrong. If this should become the case, you should seek some professional consultation.

One of the things that drives many parents batty is to see their child do something (bad) that other children don't seem to do, or else see other children do something good that their own child does not do. We call this the *"Shirley's child (does or) doesn't do that"* syndrome. If you see a neighbor's child share a toy, and your child never does, you may go home and start to "practise" sharing with your child ("here, take it . . . now give it back"), for three straight hours. If your child bit you on the arm, and you don't know of any other child that has bitten her parent, you're apt to be more upset, more severe with your child, and to view her other behavior as similarly dastardly. The truth of the matter is this: if Shirley's child didn't bite – and Shirley may not have been telling the truth, or she may not be around often enough to know (ask the nanny or daddy) – then you can be sure that Shirley's child scratched, kicked, threw toys, or all of the above. It is not wise to judge your child's behavior solely by the happenstance observations of other children (or by asking their parents). *Knowledge*, about what children normally do and don't do, is the best way to prepare yourself to be the best parent you can.

2

WHEN ARE WE (PARENTS) PART OF THE PROBLEM AND PART OF THE SOLUTION?

Giving my child a "head start"

There is nothing at all wrong with wanting to give your child a "head start." At the same time, however, it is not good to be a "pushy" parent, to force children before they're ready, to nag at them, or to provide so much structure to their day that there is little free time or quality of life for the child. While parents struggle with this dilemma – wanting to give a child every advantage (signing up for everything from music to swimming to French classes), yet not wanting to pressure or push the child too much – there is no real dilemma here. There is no real dilemma if you understand what a "head start" means.

A "head start" simply means that we are teaching our children something before the natural environment usually gives them an opportunity to learn it. For example, the typical preschool does not teach reading, arithmetic, writing, swimming, or how to play a musical instrument; it is mostly socialization, making friends, learning to be in a group, listening to a teacher, and getting along with others (although it does teach some concepts, like colors, days of the week, etc.). And yet, children are also mentally and physically ready to tackle reading, music, arithmetic, etc., and to *enjoy* these, during the preschool years. We are therefore giving our child a "head start" if we teach her (or sign up for classes that teach these skills) in the early years.

It is a "head start" by default, only because the natural community environment does not teach certain things to your child when he is ready to learn it; for some reason they wait. The focus, then, is *not* on beating or being superior to other children. Rather, the purpose is to enrich the child's world, teach her things that will increase her repertoire, freedom, and enjoyment. Viewed in this way, there is no pressure, there is nothing to push.

Don't be afraid to sign up your child for a class, but if, after attending a few times, he doesn't like it, then it is unfair – it is not beneficial – to force him to continue. If it's not fun, he won't learn much anyway; it's better to find those activities, classes, sports, or hobbies that are fun, or find a teacher who makes them fun, so the child will challenge himself, gain more and more mastery, and progress at his own pace. In this case, there will be no need to push; in fact, it will be all you can do to get him out of the pool, or away from the computer.

There is nothing inherently good or bad about classes, structure, or teaching reading to a young child . . . it depends on whether the child likes it or not. If a child enjoys zooming from one class to the next, with her whole weekend planned, so be it; if not, cancel them (or try a different teacher). This is not to say we shouldn't teach reading or swimming because the child doesn't take to it immediately. Rather, it is to say that we must make it fun, be creative in our teaching, or else it will be an upsetting experience for parent and child, something both parties dread, and the child will learn slowly, if at all.

I thought it was valuable for my child to learn to read during the preschool years, for two reasons. First, I thought he would enjoy it once he got far enough along to use it – reading signs at the park, words in his favorite book, etc. Second, it would give him a "head start" in school, in the sense that he would be prepared for a wider range of educational opportunities than a child who was not reading yet.

I knew, however, that if I sat down with a bunch of letters and drilled him, he would avoid it at all costs. Instead, I always did it during a story, while at the park, or during play, so it was a part of enjoyable activities. I did it a little here, a little there, stopping whenever he got tired of it. And I always used "natural" enjoyable things to teach with: while reading a story, during an exciting part, I'd stop for a second and ask him what letter this was, what sound it made (i.e. "P"), and then say, "That's right, great!" (if he was right) or "It's a 'P'" (if he didn't know), and then tell him the word ("Pow"). Then I'd go on with the story, stopping only now and then to ask the same or another letter. As your child progresses, you will find that he recognizes letters on the street, in the park, on TV, in the comics, in other stories, on licence plates, and that he prides himself on knowing it. As your child starts to master more letters and sounds, and begins to sound out simple words (mom, dad, toy, stop, etc.), you will find that he enjoys it, that he does it on his own in other situations, and that he asks you "what word is this" when he is interested to know.

The important thing is not to rush it, not to push, to do it just as long as the child is enjoying it and to stop if it interferes instead with the story (his enjoyment). If it is not a pressure situation, if it is not a drill, then the child will learn, gradually. This is giving your child a "head start," simply because it widens the child's horizons and enriches his world. It is not good if it is forced because the child will come to hate reading and develop all kinds of avoidance behavior (whining, oppositional behavior, delay tactics and distractions, etc.) to get out of it.

High expectations

We all want our child to be bright, popular, athletic, truthful, and socially skillful. And these are, of course, good things. But we must be careful always to keep asking ourselves whether what we want, what we expect, what we are asking of our child, is for our benefit or theirs.

Many parents are particularly sensitive about their own weaknesses, and expect (even demand) that a child excel where the parent is weak. If you're too fat, you may be hypersensitive about your child's weight and what he eats. If you want to be more popular, you may watch and try to guide the child's every move when she is with other children. If you're an armchair quarterback, you may practise football and "see" extraordinary potential in your child, and expect extraordinary performance.

We must be aware that in such situations it is our problem, not the child's. It really doesn't matter if the child does not take to sports, or is not particularly good at soccer. Very few children are very tactful, sharing, considerate, or skilled at making friends and influencing people, but most children do have at least a few friends, and care about those friends.

We can still teach the child in these areas, help her to improve (using the principles described in Part 3 of this book). We can in fact have expectations, and help the child to excel. But we must have reasonable expectations; we must not be disappointed if the child meets some and not others (which is of course inevitable). We must help the child to learn, in a positive and enjoyable way, rather than constantly pushing her, pressuring him, to do more, to do it better.

Competition with other parents

When we had our first child, I watched him like a hawk. I compared him to other children, and myself to other parents. Parenting was new and scary; I wanted to be good at it. I saw other parents who seemed to do things with their child that I couldn't.

I quickly learned how foolish it was to compete with other parents and children. There will always be another child who's smarter than yours, more mature, seems to obey his parents more, doesn't use "silly talk," speaks three languages, or learns calculus at three days of age. To judge yourself, your child, and your ability as a parent, in this way, is a losing proposition. You can't win. Moreover, there *is* nothing to win.

If you see a parent who has thought of a clever way to teach swimming, ask her about it, and try to adopt it. It does no good to be jealous of that parent, or the skills of her child. It does some good to learn from others, to use their experience to improve yourself and help teach your child.

I remember so many times, when getting together with other families, parents who would subtly launch into their child, tickle her, show off what she could do, show 600 ways they could make their child laugh. It was as though they had to demonstrate what great parents they were, first, before they could just relax and let the children go play together.

It's natural for this to occur with the first child, during the first year. But, in fact, it's pure silliness, something parents should leave behind as soon as possible. It is good to watch how other parents interact with their child, to ask them how they taught their child to read or swim, to share notes and thoughts on the difficult task of putting a sobbing, pleading child to bed; but it does no good to compete with that parent, to pit your child against theirs. Vanity and competition not only has no place in child-rearing, it detracts from and can take all the pleasure out of being a parent. Moreover, just because their child walks, talks, or swims before yours does not make those parents smarter or better – on the contrary, it is the person who listens, watches, and learns, rather than talking or showing off, who is really the smarter parent.

Handling a child's relationship with your spouse

At certain times, a child can seem closer to one parent than another, and this can be difficult for a parent to deal with. When your first child is born, a couple often decides whether one partner will stop work to care for the newborn. Often, it is the mother – since she has just been through a pregnancy and will be at home for a while anyway: she is breast-feeding, and she can take a maternity leave – although the father is now taking on this role, or at least sharing the responsibility, more than ever before.

If mom does stay at home, even for just a maternity leave, she has more time (and of course more responsibility) for the child, and they become closer, faster. The child becomes more dependent on mom than on dad, and seems more upset when mom leaves the room than when dad leaves. In the evening, mom tells dad about all the new, special things the child did that day. Dad can feel left out, even jealous of the close relationship and time that mom has with junior. It is a time for mom to be sensitive to dad's role and dad's needs. It is also a time for dad to realize that

he too can have a strong relationship with that child, if he takes
the time (evenings and weekends) to develop it. Dad must realize that his relationship with the child can be different from
mom's, but just as strong. And dad must realize that a
relationship is not set or finalized in the first year, that there is
lots of time, that the child's dependency will be at times on him
and at times on mom. Most of all, dad must keep his perspective
– after all, the most important thing is that the child is developing a strong family relationship, that mom is doing such an important thing for the child and the family. It is important that this
happens, that the child is loved and cared for, not who gets to do
it how much. Parents should decide who will do what for the
child, how the responsibility will be shared, so that each has a
role. And they should continue talking about it, so that
responsibilities can be adjusted to suit the changing needs of
mom, dad, and the baby.

Beginning in the second or third year, the child begins to identify with the same-sex parent. A boy starts imitating dad more
than mom, dressing like him, wanting to go with him to work,
and taking part in his recreational activities. If the child is a boy,
it can be difficult for mom, especially if she stayed home to care
for that child. She labored over every whim, whine, scrape, and
feeding – the child was so dependent on her. Then one day, she
realizes that the child is looking to dad a bit more, wanting to be
with him, wanting to be like him. Since dad is away much more
of the time, it may be special to the child when he is home, and
the child may spend most of his time "choosing" dad when both
mom and dad are home. This can be difficult for mom. It can be
especially difficult if mom has let go of her work, hobbies, leisure
activities, and social interests during the past two years to take
care of that child. She may have seen her role, her self-esteem,
rest almost solely in taking care of that child, and have little else
to fall back on.

During this time, dad needs to be sensitive to mom's needs,
fears, and insecurities. Mom needs some outside interests, time
to pursue some social and recreational activities. They need to
talk together about each parent's role, and what is best for the
child. Both parents need to appreciate what the other is doing,

rather than be jealous of it. And they need to keep their perspective, be realistic, know that both parents can have an equally strong, if different, relationship to that child. Over time, the child will come to rely on mom and dad for different things, but there is no reason that child should rely, love, or depend upon one more than the other. In the final analysis, your relationship with that child will depend upon the love, time, and effort you put into it over the years, not upon whether you are the mom or dad, not upon who stayed home the first six months, and not upon who did the diapering or feeding.

The "who does he / she look like?" syndrome

It's amazing how many parents ask this question – even more amazing to see a parent's face drop if you say the child looks more like the spouse. It's almost funny to watch a parent's reaction as they get upset, put their nose (ears, lips) next to the child's, and try to convince you that if you really look closely, the child has many more of that parent's features: "How can you say that? She has a mole the same place I do; she has a nose right in the middle of her face just like mine, and her father's goes way over here. . . ."

Some parents really take it quite seriously, as if a child having more of that parent's features must therefore have more kinship, be closer, and be more like that parent in all (other) ways. Not true!

Virtually every child has features of both parents. Some features are a combination of the parents', or in between them, like skin coloring. Other features, like sex, will be like one parent or the other. But each child gets a good deal from both parents.

It's OK to ask the question (most parents will), as long as you don't attach any importance to it or ask it too often. It is simply not an important or meaningful question because a child who has 47 of mom's features and only 21 of dad's will not necessarily be more like mom, or closer to mom. Furthermore, there are many things that you can't see or compare – a child's spirit, compassion, or personality – and the shape of a child's nose in comparison is not really very telling or important. Moreover, while we may all be born with genetic predispositions toward certain behavioral styles (i.e. an active versus inactive child, an aggressive versus nonaggressive child), the literature clearly shows that these are more strongly influenced by the environment, by the family, and by what happens after birth.

A child is not born like mom or dad. All people are individuals, and all individuals are combinations of other individuals (as well as the environment they grew up in). It is important to remember this because a child will often pick up on your disappointment, learning that it is important who she looks like, and get "caught" between the parents. This can only do harm, as the child sees the competition or jealousy between the two people she loves most in the world.

The question becomes even less important when you realize that the child's features often change quite dramatically during the first six years. My first child looked very much like me during the first year – there was no doubt he had my legs, my size, my coloring, etc. By the age of four, he looked much more like my wife; in fact, he looked more like the milkman than like me!

As children grow older, their physical features become less salient as their personality develops. It is the personality, energy, and spirit of the child that determine what she is like. And in most cases, both parents will be surprised at the things that child does – the child will become an individual in her parents' eyes, a person, not like anyone else in the world. If you realize this early on, that a child is unique, that what she is like will be determined more by her personality than by her nose, then we can avoid those little upsets for parents (and children) by not taking seriously the question "Who does she look like?"

Sibling rivalries

The issue of sibling rivalry comes up as soon as a second child is born. The older child will no longer be center stage all the time, as there is now another child to care for. Mom in particular will have her hands full for a while between caring for the newborn and recuperating from the delivery. Dad, too, will want to spend time with the new baby. Your first child can feel left out, jealous of the new sibling and all the attention she's getting.

There are several ways to help prevent sibling rivalries. Before the child is even born, you can talk about her, and the new pleasures she will bring *to your child* (a new playmate; she'll love you so much; she'll bring new toys; you'll be a big brother now, a big boy; etc.). You can read stories about it, discuss names for the baby together, involve the child in planning the care of the newborn – "Will you help me feed her (hold the bottle, play with her, take her out in the stroller, change her diaper, teach her how to use the toys, tickle her)?" We should prepare the child as much as possible, by talking about the newborn, feeling her kick in mommy's stomach, and telling him she is *his* sister (not "the parents'" child).

When the child is born, and dad takes junior to see mommy and the baby at the hospital, it is often helpful to have a surprise or present ready *from the newborn* to your older child. We did this each day, and it really got the relationship off to a very positive beginning. "Oh, Benjamin, Rebecca has a present for you. She loves you so-o-o much. Isn't it great to have a sister?" When he came to see the baby in the hospital, we talked to him about her, what he was like when he was a baby, and asked him to do things for her.

It is helpful if dad makes sure to spend a lot of time with the older child, both while mom is in the hospital and for a while after she gets home. In this way, the child will feel he is still getting lots of attention. During this time, you should include him as much as possible in caring for, holding (with your help), kissing, diapering, and tickling the baby, etc. This accomplishes two things. First, of course, it helps to establish a relationship between the children early. Second, it will teach him about the baby's needs, so he will understand at a later time when you say: "I have to change the baby's diaper first, and then I can play."

As the new baby grows, it is very important to include, encourage, and praise the older child for his positive interactions with the baby. "Hey, Benjamin, can you make Rebecca laugh?" When he does (or tries), he should be praised lavishly ("How did you do that? I couldn't do that. She must like you an awful lot;

look how she's watching you. What a great brother you are!"). In no time, you will find that he enjoys making her laugh, and will go to great lengths to get her cackling. In the same way, when she begins to make sounds, we can show the older child how much fun it is to imitate the baby, and clap for her when she imitates us. We can together show her how to "dance," how to make happy or silly faces, and revel when she tries to do it. As the young child grows, you will find them doing more and more together, engaging in new and different activities.

There will of course come a time when the older child (accidentally or otherwise) stabs the baby with his toy sword, pushes her, or otherwise acts negatively toward her. This can be dealt with as a problem of aggression, tantrums, or sharing (see Part 4 for the handling of these), and does not necessarily imply a sibling rivalry. On the other hand, when you hear "She took *my* toy," and it was not a toy that he was playing with at the time, then it does suggest some rivalry. In this case, you can make sure that he in fact has some toys that are strictly his, and let him choose them. Beyond that, he must learn to share, to be fair, especially with his sister. We can say, "OK, which toy do you want to play with? – Rebecca can play with some you're not using," and then stand firm in letting the baby use toys that the older child is not using. By giving him some choice, some control, it usually takes some of the sting out of it (her using his toys), but the choice he is given is only which toy he wants, not whether she can in fact use some of the toys.

There are two other approaches to dealing with the situation when the older child feels the baby is intruding. First, we can join them, if necessary, to start a game or activity that involves both of them. "Hey, Benjamin, watch this. I'm going to put a towel over my head, pull it off, and play Peek-a-Boo with her . . . look at her laugh . . . she's reaching for the towel! Let's put it on her head now and see what happens, OK? Do you want to do it? . . . Wow, she pulled the towel off your head! She's crawling toward you, for more . . . Boy, does she love you. What a great brother you are!" In this way, we can steer the situation into a positive one, and minimize any negative thoughts or feelings between them.

A second approach is simply to distract him. "Hey, Benjamin, do you want to see if Adam wants to come over (play a game, help me cook, go to John's house, cut out an airplane, finger paint, etc.)?" The two children can't always play together, and we can try to help the older child find other enjoyable things to do.

Sharing parental responsibilities

Most parents talk about who's going to do what before the first child is born. Most parents never talk about it again.

No one can anticipate how difficult and draining it can be to take care of children, or to perform a balancing act between job and family. Moreover, people change over time, our wants and needs change, and our responsibilities change (grow) without our even realizing it. Over the years, there may be additional children: each needs to be taken to this class and that doctor, and you can't turn off the responsibilities at five o'clock.

Parents need to *continue* to talk about who should be responsible for what. The responsibilities change dramatically over the years, and there will be times when each parent feels overburdened.

I used to wonder what my wife did with her day, jealous that she got to stay home while I had to face the hard cruel world out there. She didn't have the tremendous stresses I felt at work, even if she did work hard. Then, I stayed home to take care of the kids for a few days, while my wife flew off to attend a funeral. I thought I was going to die. I couldn't wait for the kids to go to bed. All the zest, energy, and creativity I tried so hard to spend on "quality time" during evenings and weekends became laughable ivory-tower inanities when I had the kids 24 hours a day. There were no lunch breaks, coffee breaks, time to sit and think without distraction. There was no parents' union, no place to file a grievance. When she got back, I was the most loving, doting, appreciative husband you ever saw.

It was a good lesson, an important lesson. As discussed in Part 3 (see "Quality of Life"), it is very valuable to "walk a mile in your (spouse's) shoes" before you complain about your own responsibilities. It was just as true that my wife was quite averse to taking over my responsibilities, so we were closing in on a balance.

It doesn't matter who does what, which parent has more or less responsibility for bringing in the money, which one drives the kids to preschool. What is important is that all the jobs get done, and both parents feel they are fairly distributed, that *they are appreciated*. It is important that the parents continue to talk about these responsibilities, that they understand what the other is going through. In this way, new responsibilities can be shared, both parents get some time to themselves, both parents are able to maintain at least some outside interests, and we can appreciate what each other does, why our spouse is at times preoccupied, upset or ill-tempered, and help each other through the tough times.

Yelling/fighting in front of the children

All of us get upset at times, need to blow off steam, argue with our spouse. It's normal; it's human.

At the same time, it can be difficult for children to see this. These two people are practically his whole world, his home base, his Rocks of Gibraltar. To see them fight can be a very upsetting experience, quickly reducing most children to tears.

The best approach, I think, is to be sensitive to the child, to minimize the fighting as much as possible. This is not what we want to model; rather, we want to show him how to *discuss* things (not yell), how to work out disagreements. If you feel yourself getting angry, it is probably better to go somewhere else to argue, or to put the matter on hold if possible until the kids are otherwise occupied (in bed, in another room, outside). This will not always be possible, of course, but if we are sensitive to the effects that fighting can have on our kids, we can often handle the situation in another way or at another time.

If marital arguments are a constant, daily occurrence, then the problem is bigger and self-control alone may not be enough. It may indicate some fundamental problems in the marriage, and the parents should face them, talk about them, and get some help (i.e. marital counselling) if they feel the marriage is not a happy one.

Separation and divorce

This is not a happy situation for anyone involved, and there is no way that I know of to prevent the pain. We can, however, minimize it as much as possible.

If two parents are not happy together, and their differences are irreconcilable, then it does no good to stay together "for the children." The fighting, arguing, and lack of affection between them will be a bad model for the child. He will be constantly upset by the fighting. There may be competition between the parents for the child's affection, a tendency to "spoil" him and shower him with affection, and, as a result, no one is willing to be firm, to be the disciplinarian. The literature shows that the actual separation between parents has much less effect on the child than the fighting and animosity that led up to the separation.

There may be some bad feelings between the parents, and of course they will have their own thoughts and feelings to deal with. Even so, they still need to talk about their future responsibilities for the child. How this is handled will go a long way in determining how upset the child will be about the situation. It is not just the division of property, living arrangements for the child, "visiting rights," or payments for the child's clothes that are at issue. The parents each need to explain to the child in a positive way what is happening, assure her of their love, and if at all possible give her some choice regarding where she wants to be and what she wants to do on Saturdays, etc. She needs to see the parents together, being friendly if at all possible. The parents need to talk about the child together, and continue talking – about what they will discipline, about competing for the child's affections, about what the child is feeling. They need to communicate *more* because they need to provide some consistency in handling the child, and to reaffirm the importance and "goodness" of *both* parents, etc.

Daycare versus nanny versus a parent staying at home: quantity versus quality of time with your child

Many parents want to work, yet feel guilty about not being with their child all day, especially during the early years. There is no reason for this guilt. Parents do not and should not live solely for their children. They must consider their own wants and needs, and not feel guilty about doing so.

At the same time, of course, parents have an obligation to their child, and that obligation is in no way lessened by the fact that they both work. (If that obligation is not enjoyable, or something they both relish, then it is questionable whether they should have children.) Assuming it is an obligation that the parents do want, then there are several ways to meet it.

There is nothing inherently good or bad about a nanny, daycare, or a parent staying at home. How good or bad it is will depend upon the nanny you get, the quality of the daycare, and whether a parent wants to be at home. The quality of the care is more important than who does it.

This does not, however, mean that all responsibility for a child can be given to a nanny or daycare, no matter how good they are. Parents will still need to establish a quality relationship with their child, make decisions about discipline, toilet training, and so on. Consequently, parents should still take an active role, both in directing and communicating with the nanny or daycare, and in making sure that "quality" time is set aside for themselves each day to spend with the child.

Many parents stay home with the child, but really don't spend much of that time talking with, reading to, or playing with that child. Much of the time together is spent meeting the child's needs – diapering, feeding, etc. – and much of the time is spent doing errands, chores, or even resting. In truth, it may not really matter very much who does these things. It is the cuddling, talking, playing, tickling – it is the time when you are attending solely to your child and she to you – that is the quality time, the interactions that will "bond" parent and child. It is very important that this time be preserved and guarded jealously. It is less important who handles the other responsibilities.

Some parents can feel guilty, even jealous, if the nanny develops a strong relationship with the child. Deep down, they think, "It should be me; I'm the mother." On the contrary, you should be disappointed in that nanny if she does *not* develop such a relationship with your child – you would want to get a new nanny. It is *healthy* for a child to have a good, close relationship with several people, and in no way, shape, or form will it diminish your relationship with that child. If you spend the time and energy, you will have a "special" relationship with your child; if you don't, you won't. What kind of relationship a nanny has will have no bearing whatsoever on your relationship with your child. The better the nanny's relationship, the happier your child will be and the more he will learn, grow, and progress.

Can there be too much love?

No, there is never too much love for a child. There can, however, be other problems which on the surface look like too much love.

Some parents dote on, spoil, and refuse to reprimand or discipline children. This is not a question of love, for it takes effort and love to care enough to discipline a child. It does the child no good to serve his every whim, to always subordinate your own needs to his. And it is a lack of knowledge, not love, that perpetuates it.

Some parents drop all outside interests and activities to devote their time solely to their children. Having a child is of course very demanding, very time-consuming . . . and, yet, each parent should maintain some outside interests and goals. One's self-worth should not be tied up solely in the children (though of course it will always be important). Those children will go away to school, get married, have their own children, move thousands of miles away, or perhaps just grow pink beards, shave their heads, and join a commune. They're not babies for long; they'll become less dependent on you, and they'll have different interests, goals, and values. We'll never stop loving them, but we must love other things, other people, too, or else we will be overly dependent upon our children while they are becoming less and less dependent upon us.

Some parents foster dependence in their children, as if to ensure that that child will forever be their loving dutiful (and ever-present) baby. The parent may keep the child nearby almost all the time, disdaining playmates, preschool, etc. The parent may demand to do everything for the child, jealously guarding that role. That parent is not helping the child, as the child's socialization, play skills, relationships, sharing, and the ability to get along with others, will be sorely lacking.

Some parents love their child very much, but don't know that there can be a wrong time to show love and affection. When a child has a tantrum, cries because you won't come back into her bedroom at night for the twelfth time, or hits another child, it is not a time to show affection, hold her or tell her you love her. This is dealt with extensively in Parts 3 and 4 of this book, and will not be reviewed again here. The point here is that this is *not* a function of how much you love a child, it is a matter of knowing how to help or teach that child. The parent who knows when to praise a child, and when to withhold affection, does not love that child less – that parent is simply more knowledgeable about how to help and teach that child.

When you like one child better than another

All children are not equal. One child may be brighter, one cuter, one more outgoing, one more sensitive . . . and we as parents, as people, may find one or another of these qualities more attractive. Parents can be more attracted to one child than the other(s), and there's nothing wrong with that.

It is wrong, however, and potentially harmful to the "other" children, if one child is treated very differently. If you are always praising and attending to one child, and ignoring the others, then it will inevitably bring about problems between the children as well as between the "nonfavorites" and the parent. While parents may be a bit more attracted to one, they should be careful to be fair in their time and treatment with all their children.

For most families, one child will be "special" at a certain time, in a certain situation, for something unusual or pleasant she did. At other times, in other situations, you will feel the same way about the other children. In most families, all the children are special, just special in different ways. What is important is not whether you are attracted to one child a bit more than the others, but whether you in fact like and love all the children. If they each are made to feel special, in their own way and at their own times, then it will not matter very much if in fact it happens a little more to one child than the other.

It is good to remember that it is much more important – for them – that they like each other. This is much more important than who you like best. They are peers, in the same generation, and will be counting on each other, needing each other, long after the parents are gone. While we as parents feel a tremendous bond to our children, and expect that relationship to last throughout our lifetimes, it is wise to remember that the love, the foundation, any sense of family and belonging we give them, will survive in the relationship they have with each other – and only begins with the relationship they have with us. If we treat one child – a "favorite" – too differently, we jeopardize all of these relationships, and the very foundation we are trying to give our children.

3

HOW PARENTS CAN HELP
THEIR CHILD: PRINCIPLES

Overview

The principles described here are general "laws of human behavior," and their use is not restricted to when a child's behavior becomes a "problem." These are in fact principles of
child-rearing, useful no matter what it is you would like to help,
change, or teach. They are principles that should be adopted, as
much as possible, into the very fabric of all parent-child interactions and relationships.

Even if there is no problem whatsoever, you can still encourage and teach new social, verbal, play, and intellectual skills.
These principles are therefore useful in teaching most *anything*
you want to teach – curiosity, creativity, reading, courtesy, sen-
sitivity, etc. Teaching numbers, letters, and colors; teaching a
child to say "please" and "thank-you"; teaching the names of
people or the names of clothes (pants, shirts, shoes); teaching
morals, or simply rules for around the house; teaching a child
how to dress himself or act in church; all can be accomplished
using these principles. These are, simply, principles of learning.

Demonstrating for your child ("Modelling")

The fastest way to teach a child something is to model it for
him, to demonstrate it. For example, if my child wants another
child's toy, then we'll look for a toy to trade. I go with my child to
pick out a favorite wham-bang sure-fire special toy that no child

36

could resist. We go over to the other child, play with the toy in front of her (to show that it's new and interesting), and then I offer to trade with that child. In this way, my child is learning how to handle that situation the next time it comes up. If I ask him to write the letter "B," I don't just provide pencil and paper. I draw the first "B" and ask him to do the second one, or to trace mine (and, of course, I praise his first efforts).

It's amazing how much they can learn from modelling. I keep a computer at home, and my child can now make it dance. At first, he just learned what the "return" key did, then the "escape" key, then the "arrow" keys, then how to put a disk in, how to turn on the machine, and then off we went to different software packages. If they are really interested in something – sports, computers, reading, etc. – modelling can be used to teach incredibly elaborate, even sophisticated, skills.

It is much more effective than just using instructions. A child (or adult) learns more slowly, with many more mistakes along the way, if we only *explain* how to do it. Modelling it, demonstrating, is a much faster way of teaching, whether you're trying to establish social skills, play, or speech. In fact, no matter what you're trying to teach, modelling should be included if at all possible.

Prompting and guiding a child

A "prompt" is any extra help we use to guide learning in a child. For example, to help a child pick out a "coat" from other clothing, we can put it closer, make it larger that the other things, or even remove the other things altogether (at first, so he can't help but pick the right thing). In these ways, the child is more apt to get it right. Later, we gradually remove our help (the prompt), by moving it back toward the other clothes (now he can't just pick the closest item), or we can add just one other article of clothing (i.e. shoes next to the coat), for him to choose from (then two, three and four pieces of clothing).

In general, we make the task easy at first, by giving some extra help, and then we fade out that help ("prompt-fading"). If a child can't find the letter "B," I might make it the only one that is underlined, or I might have an arrow pointing to it, or make the "B" larger than the other letters. These (underlining, pointing, size) are prompts. When the child gets it right four or five times with the prompt, then I reduce the help I gave him a bit – the size, underlining, or arrow can be made slightly smaller. If he does OK here, I reduce the help again . . . and again . . . until I'm eventually giving him no help at all – I say, "Where's the 'B'?" and he picks it out and gives it to me.

Sometimes a prompt need not be very elaborate. If a child asks how to open a briefcase, you can just say "push the gold bars up." Or we can just say, "In the hamper, please," or "Over there," if he throws his dirty clothes on the floor instead of in the hamper. Perhaps we need only point to the sink if he forgets to wash his hands after going to the bathroom.

Sometimes, we can use modelling itself as a prompt. For example, my son loves dinosaurs, so we bought a few books and paper cut-outs of dinosaurs. I'd ask him, "Who's this?" and of course he wouldn't remember. So I'd help him by saying (modelling), "Tyrannosaurus Rex." The next time this dinosaur appeared in a story or a game, I would again ask: "Who is this?" If he needed help, I would just say, "Tyranno . . ." giving him only as much help as he needed to get it right. Soon, I found he would get it right when I only said, "T-t-t . . ." and then of course he got it right completely on his own.

There are an infinite number of ways to help (prompt) a child, and almost anything can be taught this way – getting dressed, swimming, sports, sharing, speech, courtesy, and so on. In putting on a child's pants, we can do it all for him (helping him is the prompt) except for the zipper, which he must zip up himself. When this is easy, we require him to pull up his pants *and* do the zipper. When he's got this, we let him put his legs in, pull up the pants, and zip the zipper. In this case, the amount we are doing for him is the prompt or help, and as the child gets better at it we gradually reduce the amount of help.

Parents must be careful not to teach things that children are not yet ready for. If it is too hard, or the child is not yet sufficiently coordinated, then the task will become frustrating, upsetting, and negative. For example, buttoning is one of the most difficult of dressing skills for young children, and need not be taught until the child can otherwise fully dress himself. No matter how much fun you make it, if he's not physically mature or coordinated enough, he cannot learn it.

However, if the child is not ready for a task yet, that does not mean we stop helping or teaching. For example, if a child is not able to dress himself, we can work on undressing, which is much easier. And we can, of course, use prompt-fading principles for this new, easier, task. For example, we can take off all his clothes, pull his shirt to the top of his head, and let him just pull it off. Later, we can take his arms out of his sleeves for him, and then let him pull his shirt all the way off. Then, we can take one arm out of the sleeve, letting him take out the other and pull his shirt off. Continuing in small steps, we can easily teach him to take his shirt, pants, socks, and shoes off, and put them in the hamper.

In all prompting situations, of course, the child is richly praised when he gets it right (even though you helped, with a "prompt"); if he is wrong a couple of times, we use a greater prompt (i.e. more help).

Breaking down a goal into smaller steps ("Task analysis")

Task analysis simply means that we should break our goals down into smaller steps, and teach them one at a time. In many cases, it is impossible to teach the goal all at once – tying shoelaces, drawing the letter "A," finding her way to the playground, telling you his address or phone number. These (and many, many other skills) can, however, be taught if we break them down into smaller steps and teach them one at a time. In the case of tying shoelaces, we can do it all for her except the last step – letting her just pull or tighten the loops. Then we can teach her to put one loop underneath the other and pull; then teach her to make the loops, put one under the other and pull; and so on.

Similarly, in teaching a child to make an "A," we might draw all of it except for the middle line, which she will do. When she's accomplished this, we leave two lines off for her to do, and so on. An alternative is to let her trace an "A" that is made up of a series of dots, and we can gradually reduce the number of dots until she is finally printing an "A" all by herself (no dots).

In teaching a child how to get to the playground, school, or a friend's house, we might walk with him all the way a number of times. Then, we ask him which way to go when we're only one block away. Then we stop two blocks away, and ask him where we go (at each block). Then we stop three blocks away, and ask him which way to go (at each block). If at any time he doesn't know, or makes a mistake, then of course we show him the right way – but for the next few days we stop at the same place so that he can practise the right way, and master it, before adding more to the task (stopping four blocks away).

Praise and attention

B etween the ages of six months to six years, the major source of pleasure in a child's world is the attention and praise of his parents. Children will go to any length to get it. They may beg ("Please, oh please, daddy, let's play"); hide the tie, food, or shoes you are looking for; jump in your lap and smother you with hugs and kisses; or hit, stab, shoot, or beam you up to the playroom, in order to get some personal attention. They will try anything and everything, from saying, "I'm so-o-o sad," to suggesting *your* favorite game ("Let's play chess").

In many ways, it's a wonderful time. The kids are dependent on us, and they don't hide it one bit. Therefore, our parenting instincts – loving, caring for, and helping children – are easy to fulfill, because the child is constantly asking for us. You will like this period (usually), because you will be made to feel quite special by that child.

In general, the literature clearly shows that a *child continues to do things that bring him praise and attention.* They *love* that attention. So, when she's alone, and yells for us to come, if we do come running what do you think will happen the next time she's alone and wants company? Of course, she'll scream. And scream louder, if you don't come running fast enough, and eventually add a little foot-stomp here and a toy-throw there for some emphasis. On the other hand, if I "catch" my child sharing a toy with a friend, and I go over and say, "Oh, Benjamin, I'm so-o-o proud of you (hug). You shared your toy, and that's what big boys do," then he will want to share again (and may well offer another toy right then and there). After a while, regularly praising the special things that children do, you will find that your child comes running into the kitchen, saying, "Look, mommy, I shared my toy with Greta. Come see." He will begin to internalize this, learn that it is good, right, something that deserves to be applauded.

There are two important points to be gleaned from this. First, we must realize how very motivating our praise and attention is. The child couldn't care less whether it comes from good behavior or bad behavior, as long as he gets the attention. It will strengthen and support *any* type of behavior – good or bad. Good parenting, then, demands that we look for, praise, and attend to the good things that children do, while making sure to minimize our interactions, and forget about praise, when the child is behaving in some way that is unacceptable.

This is the easiest, and yet the most powerful way, to help our children. But we must look for opportunities! We must look for things to praise. If you do, the behavior you praise will grow, flourish, become a strong part of the child's personality and make-up. If we ignore the good things they do, they may just stop doing them.

Some parents have a difficult time showing emotion, and rarely use praise with anyone. They should be encouraged to practise it, perhaps trying it when alone with the child. The nice thing is *praise brings its own rewards*, as the child in turn asks for you more, listens to you more, and loves you more. That parent will naturally find himself soon using praise and attention all over the place, in new and creative ways, for a whole host of child accomplishments.

When praise is richly used, we find less problem behavior, fights, nagging, tantrums, noncompliance, etc., in the home. Why? It's simple. When a home is rich in love and warmth, then the absence of that love can be very upsetting. It becomes *much* easier to deal with a tantrum because showing disapproval – the stoppage in play and conversation, the warmth that has gone out of daddy's eyes, the firmness in mommy's voice and posture – is in stark contrast to the love and attention the child usually gets. He will quickly stop doing things that lead to your disapproval. In short, the liberal use of praise and attention *makes your reprimand much more effective*, and we don't have to use reprimands (or punishment) nearly as often.

The importance of praise cannot be overemphasized. It makes learning fun. Without it, there will be little motivation for a child to learn the things you want to teach. With it, the child will persevere, and he will feel good about what he has done. He will enjoy learning, and try harder. It will be "fun" instead of "work." If we make a game out of it, if we use praise, if we do it together (attention) rather than just telling a child to do it (or waiting for him to do it on his own), the child will enjoy it. Many people simply don't take the time to do it *with* their child, to praise and encourage his efforts, notice his nuances and each small gain. As a result, the child doesn't participate . . . and doesn't learn.

The importance of feedback

Feedback is absolutely crucial to learning – any kind of learning. It is the feedback that tells a child whether he's doing it right or if it can be better. Feedback means that we make an evaluative comment, and correct the behavior as needed: "way to go"; "that was great"; "awright"; or, if it isn't quite right: "almost perfect, we just need to do up this button, too"; "very close, but let's try it again and give Elizabeth your new toy *before* you take hers, OK?"

The feedback must always be related *specifically to the behavior* – what was good or not so good about it. It is *never* a comment about the child, just about the behavior. We can say that a behavior was done wrong, but never that a *child* is wrong. We focus on the behavior for two reasons: it is the behavior that can be improved, and feedback (with praise) will help to do that; and second, we never want to give the child the impression that he or she is wrong, bad, dumb, or otherwise inadequate – it is the behavior that wasn't right, and it is the behavior that can be made right. We don't want inappropriate behavior in one area to cast a large ugly shadow over the child and all his other behavior.

Feedback is always helpful, but particularly so when a child is having some difficulty. If he is not usually very nice to friends, then we can start to give feedback on many of the good and not so good things he does: "I loved the way you shared the closet when playing hide-and-seek"; "I think Johnny cried because you pushed him – so let's go over together to say I'm sorry."

The more skillful a child becomes in an area – whether it be sports or sharing or toiletting – the less feedback he will need. Feedback is primarily useful when the child is learning something new, or learning something not to do (i.e. tantrums or aggression). When she is in the process of learning, feedback will guide her and ensure the fastest learning; at the same time, it will minimize frustration, as she won't repeat the same mistakes over and over.

Finally, feedback should always be paired with praise when the child does well. It is not enough to say, "You made an 'A' correctly." It sounds "cold," doesn't it? He may do it correctly, but he may never do it again. On the other hand, if we add praise, "You made a perfect 'A'; that's wonderful. Let's show it to mommy," then he will want to do more letters – and, more importantly, he will feel good about what he has done, what he has accomplished and learned, and that he persevered. He will enjoy learning and try harder. It will be "fun," instead of "work."

Behavior problems as language: what is your child telling you?

Much of what a child *does* – good or bad – is communicative: it's telling you something. So we must "listen to what a child does." It is important to understand why the child is behaving that way if we are to do something about it, change it, and teach more appropriate ways to behave.

There are many possible reasons why a child might be behaving inappropriately, but two of them are by far the most common and deserve special attention (others are discussed in Part 4 as we describe each of the child behaviors individually).

First, a child will try almost anything to get his way. This does not mean that children are cold, conniving or sneaky, rather it's just that they naturally learn (as we all do) what will get them what they want – the swing, a cookie, to play a little longer, to go this way when you want to go that way. Oftentimes, what they want is just attention – someone to sit beside them, to play, to just notice them, or to hold their hand while watching TV or going to sleep. They will in fact dominate your every waking minute, *demanding* your attention, if they had their druthers.

Sometimes parents want to do these things with them, and sometimes we just don't have the time or energy. This is when children will try "new" things to get their way. They may yell, scratch, bite, stomp, hit, plead, or pout if they don't get their way, or don't get their way fast enough. They may throw a vase, a toy, food, or a shoe – and they don't know that the vase is sentimental or valuable, and that you'd prefer they broke something cheap. They may go airborne headfirst off the sofa, climb on your head, or put their finger in your ear, nose or mouth, if you dare to be preoccupied.

It's usually easy to tell what they want, if we take the time to notice. In fact, they'll usually tell you or show you. They may say, "Let's play," take you by the hand to the toys, or hand over a puppet for you to bring to life. Or he may just laugh when he sees you jump from a karate kick to the shins. They don't want any confusion; they want to help you understand what it is they're after, so their message (smiling, gestures, yelling, pleading, kicking, etc.) is usually quite clear.

The problem is, the more extreme the behavior the better the chance that it will get our attention. It's hard not to notice. (And for the first two years or so, we were in fact quite attentive to every whine and whisper.) The child has learned to cry and yell to get service. And he quickly learns that there are other new and effective ways (whining, tantrums, aggression, oppositional behavior, pleading, etc.) to get our attention.

A *second* major motivator for young children is to *avoid* doing things they don't like to do. Whether it's going to bed, getting dressed, taking medicine, eating when she'd rather play, going out when she'd rather stay in, or staying in when you'd rather go out, children will try all the same misbehavior to avoid the calamity. And they'll make up a few more – pretending they didn't hear, hiding, or just turning their head so you can't see them pick their nose or cross their eyes when you've told them not to.

It is crucial to understand why the child is doing this – what the behavior "says" – because the reasons for the behavior will determine how to handle it. In general, if we understand why the child is doing it, we can make sure misbehavior does not pay off, and we can teach him alternative, appropriate behavior that will. But we can only do this if we are sensitive to what the child is after, what he really wants.

If he wants attention, then of course we must be careful not to start a game, a discussion, or a hugfest if he misbehaves to get it. On the other hand, if he is trying to avoid something – putting on his jacket or shoes, going to bed, wearing "that" shirt – then it would be a mistake to ignore him because ignoring him allows the tantrum to work (he doesn't go to bed, or put on his jacket).

If we don't know what the child wants, we can't know what to do about the misbehavior, whether to ignore it or to follow through (put her jacket on, put her to bed). Moreover, we can't teach her the appropriate ways to deal with the situation if we don't know what she wants, such as appropriate ways to get your attention, or to make friends.

Punishment

Is punishment necessary?
One finger went in my eye, the others scratched down my cheek. It hurt! Without thinking, I slapped his hand and yelled, "NO!" He was crying . . . and I was trembling; it was the first time I had ever hit him, and my heart was beating a mile a minute. After a stunned moment, I gathered myself and explained to him why he couldn't do that, and what was the right way to ask me to play.

At about 1:00 a.m. I was in bed staring at the ceiling, bothered by my own impulsive, strong reaction. This had not been a thoughtful, planned strategy for dealing with the behavior – it just happened, suddenly. I was concerned at how quickly it had happened, what it might mean to him.

Finally, I was able to step back and think about what I would tell another parent who had done this. And this is what I would say: "You're not evil. You did not 'beat him up.' It was not random or arbitrary – the child did something that upset you (rather than you just being in a bad mood or taking out your frustrations on the child). Maybe you overreacted (and maybe you didn't). It will not have a lasting impact on the child or your relationship, unless it happens too frequently, or for the wrong reasons. The important thing, then, is what you learn from it."

Punishment should not be impulsive. If it is to be used, it must be used properly. There is a right way to do it and a wrong way, and doing it the wrong way can over time have serious and severe repercussions on a child. Doing it impulsively is one wrong way, and there are others. If done properly and in moderation, it is effective, and negative repercussions can be easily prevented.

This is not to suggest that it is good, or bad, to use punishment – that is an ethical issue, not a scientific one (and we will deal with the ethics of it in a minute). First, however, it is important to understand what punishment is and what it is not, when it is punishment and when it is abuse, and what are the right and wrong ways to use punishment. Only then can we talk about when and whether to use it.

What is punishment (and abuse)?

Punishment is *any negative reaction that consistently follows a misbehavior, and decreases the frequency of that misbehavior.* This definition includes several important components, all of which must be present before it can be considered punishment. It is these components that differentiate punishment from child abuse, so we will go through each of them individually in an attempt to ensure that any case of punishment is done properly.

First, the parent's reaction must be negative. While this seems obvious – and usually is – there are pitfalls. Most often, parents know what their child does not like as opposed to what he does like. But we must keep in mind that most forms of punishment include attention. For some children, attention is positive even if it is supposedly "negative attention." This is especially true of children who don't get a lot of positive attention (praise and approval, doing things together) from parents (perhaps both parents work and are often too tired at the end of the day, perhaps they feel the child should entertain himself). In these (and other) cases a child may enjoy *any* attention he can get, even nagging, yelling, screaming, or punishment (negative attention).

Some other parents accidentally combine positive and negative reactions to misbehavior. They may engage in extended discussions, feel guilty and comfort a child right after punishing him, or use a "punisher" that is not really negative to the child (sending a child to his room . . . where all his toys are; saying in a soft and gentle voice, "No, Billy, we can't do that.").

In short, if punishment is to be used, it must be a *negative* reaction – with no positive attention, comfort, soothing, or extended conversations included. We can't send mixed messages – rather, it must be a clear message, firm, and as brief as possible.

To illustrate, one of the most common (and well-researched) forms of punishment is a reprimand. Used properly, it is often effective. But I've seen parents use it incorrectly much more often than I've seen them use it correctly. For example, many parents say, "Don't do that," and that's it. This is ineffective because it's not negative, and often turns into plain old nagging ("Don't do that . . . Johnny, don't do that . . . You can't do that Johnny", and all the time the parent is in the kitchen, about 20 feet from the child, using a calm voice). Worse, the child might do it again just to get a "rise" out of mom, if mom typically gets upset at this behavior. Another common mistake occurs when parents get very upset at the child and then immediately turn around to comfort the child, taking her on their lap, holding her, calmly explaining that it wasn't that serious, it's over now, and offering to play so that they can put the episode behind them. This is a mixed message: good things happen when the child misbehaves. An effective way to use a reprimand is to suddenly grab both arms, move your face very close to his (or better yet, abruptly pull him toward you), making direct eye contact, and say "NO (hitting)," in a strong firm voice (but without yelling). Then, just let him go and do something else. No two-hour lectures, no mixed messages, no nagging, no dragging it out.

Second, punishment is any kind of negative reaction; it does *not* necessarily mean hitting, or even yelling. A stare, disapproval, a reprimand ("NO!"), is no less a punishment than slapping a child's hand – if it is negative to the child. Many children are much more upset by a reprimand which is public – in front of their friends – than a private swat on the seat of the pants (although humiliating a child has no place here, and is uncalled for). Many children are heartbroken if their parents simply disapprove: "Sheila, I can't believe you hit me." "Johnny, that was mean!" Most children are upset if you take away a toy, take them off the playground, send their friend home, or refuse to play with them because of what they did. All of these are forms of punishment; rarely is it necessary to hit a child.

A reprimand is far more effective than most people think, and usually all that will be needed if it is done properly and firmly. Most children get the message if you abruptly grab them by the (both) arms, quickly pull them toward you, bring your face inches from theirs, and say loudly, "Don't stab your sister with the sword," maintaining a serious and firm expression and voice throughout.

Third, punishment should follow the misbehavior immediately. We should not wait, or delay the punishment. Children usually think that it is whatever they did just before the punishment that was "bad." If we wait, even a few minutes, we run the risk of accidentally and unintentionally punishing something else. Suppose the child is sharing with a friend, looking at a book, or just playing by himself when you come over and say "NO HITTING!" At worst, he may stop playing, sharing, or looking at books, even though that is not what you meant to punish. At best, it will probably be a mixed and confusing message, as the child is unsure why you are doing this now, what he did wrong and when. Despite your best intentions, it is the behavior that immediately preceded the punishment that is most likely to be impacted.

Not only should punishment follow the inappropriate behavior immediately, but it should only occur when the misbehavior has occurred. We cannot react impulsively, at least not very often, and we cannot let our other moods, stresses and frustrations influence when we punish a child. If we are on edge, preoccupied, upset for some reason, we simply cannot take it out on the child. The child will have no idea what he did wrong, why he upset you so on this occasion. We must be absolutely certain to link punishment to the misbehavior so that the child can understand what he is being punished for.

Fourth, punishment must *consistently* follow the misbehavior. Nothing could be worse than to punish a behavior on one occasion, and not punish it on another. The message is very confusing to a child: he won't be sure if the behavior is bad or not; he'll "get away with it" sometimes, and spend his time figuring out when he can do it, or who will not punish it, instead of learning that it cannot be done at all.

Fifth, the rate or frequency of the (punished) behavior must decrease over time. If it does not, then something is definitely wrong – at best our reaction is ineffective, at worst it is abusive. This does not mean that the behavior must disappear for good the first time you punish it; this is rarely the case. Rather, if a child hits people two to three times per day, we must see it drop to once per day or less, and continue decreasing.

Sixth, a *warning* should always be given, for a couple of reasons. First, by saying "We have to turn off the TV in five minutes," you allow the child to anticipate and prepare for the coming change in activity; sometimes (not always) this alone can prevent a tantrum. Second, by giving a warning (i.e. "If you don't head up to bed by the time I count to three, I'll carry you up and we won't read a story"), and then following through when the warning isn't obeyed, we give the warning a special meaning. It comes to mean that it *will* be done, no matter what. After the child learns this, you will rarely face a tantrum or need to follow through in these situations. In short, the warning comes to prevent tantrums and oppositional behavior, and it will minimize the need for "follow-through."

Preventing negative side-effects of punishment
Understanding what punishment is will of course help us to do

it properly. There is more, however. There are many dangers to
using punishment, and we cannot set about just eliminating behavior in children. We must be concerned about our relationship;
we must be concerned about teaching new, alternative appropriate behavior to take the place of the behavior we are
punishing; and we must teach the child a little self-control, in a
general sense, so we don't have to continue relying on punishment to correct the child's next (mis)behavior. Here are some
simple rules to follow, which will help to ensure that punishment is used properly.

(1) *We must always ensure that there is at least three times as
much praise as there is punishment.* We never let punishment
dominate our relationship with a child. This is not what we
want to model, what we want him to learn from us. This
simple principle will ensure that love, warmth, and affection will dominate our relationship with a child. This
means, however, that when we use punishment, we must
(at other times, of course) look for other good things to
praise.

(2) *We must never just use punishment alone; we must also teach
alternative, appropriate ways for the child to interact.* It does no
good to punish a behavior unless we replace it with a better
way. If we remember that behavior is like language, that it
would be harmful to just cut off the child's communication,
then we should teach other appropriate, more effective
ways for the child to deal with the situation.

(3) *We always say "No (i.e. hitting)" when we punish.* This is
important for two reasons. First, it helps to make the message clear, so the child knows exactly what the behavior is
that you find unacceptable. Second, it pairs the verbal
command with any punishment you use, and makes that
verbal command more effective. In this way we can soon
control misbehavior verbally (and drop any other, more
severe, forms of punishment).

(4) *We use the least severe form of punishment that can be
reasonably expected to work.* There is no need for dynamite if

a firecracker will do. The real danger here is that we (parents) can easily get carried away with punishment – because it works so quickly. When my child ran out on the street after I told him not to, I gave him a swat on the rump because I felt it was dangerous and I wanted to control it *fast*! The danger is that we can become impressed with how effective that swat on the rump is, and begin to use it more as a matter of convenience rather than necessity. Such punishment – especially hitting – should be saved for urgent situations. The child gets used to even a swat on the rump if it is used too often, and it will begin to lose its effectiveness (in which case a parent has to become even more severe to have the same effect). Moreover, there are usually milder ways to punish the behavior if we take the time to look.

Positive effects of punishment

If punishment is used properly and judiciously – including all of the precautions described above – then the literature shows not only that there are no known negative effects of punishment (aside, of course, from the emotional upset of the moment), but that there are actually several possible beneficial effects.

Research shows that punishment makes your praise more effective and meaningful. If a child is never punished for inappropriate behavior, he gets used to praise and he becomes harder and harder to please; we end up moving to artificial things like money, toys, more money, bigger and more expensive toys, in order to excite him. On the other hand, if a child in some cases is punished for inappropriate behavior, it serves as a stark contrast to praise, and praise is appreciated more.

A second benefit is that punishment often increases attention and social behavior. After punishment, you will find that not only does the inappropriate behavior decrease, but the child becomes more attentive – he listens to you, watches you – and he engages in positive social behavior, such as wanting to be held, to talk, or be near you. We don't really know why. Perhaps the punishment shows to some extent that we care – that we care enough to teach and help, that we care about what the child does. Perhaps the child becomes attentive and social just to prevent further punishment. Whatever the reason, there appear to be benefits besides just stopping the (mis)behavior in question.

Third, it teaches the child what the real world is like, and how to handle it, rather than sheltering him from it (resulting in later problems of coping, sharing, stress, etc.). Even in the world of a young child, punishment does occur naturally. Children may push or hit each other, call each other names, or go to play with a different child; they may make faces, just ignore a child's requests, or leave. All of these are punishments of a sort, and unavoidable. A child cannot learn how to handle it, how to cope in the world, if we overindulge, overprotect, or otherwise shelter him from it.

Have fun with your child

In this day and age, we are finding more and more families with both parents working. And with separation and divorce a common occurrence, we are finding many single-parent households. The results are twofold: children aren't with a parent as much during the day, and when they are together the parent is often tired, preoccupied, or stressed by events at work.

In many families, parents and children simply don't have much fun together. It is hard to find the quality time. It is hard to tune out the rest of the world, relax with the child, really watch and savor the child's development. We end up talking *to* the child – as needed – rather than talking *with* the child.

The important issue is not so much how much time we spend with the child, but whether we regularly spend some "quality" time together. This is very important. And yet, our weariness at the end of a day is also quite real, and it takes a great deal of effort to play with a child when you're tired or otherwise preoccupied.

One key is to find things to do for a period of time each day that *both* the parent and the child enjoy. If it is fun for us, too, then it won't seem like "work." If it is fun for us, we will naturally continue to do it. If it is fun for both of us, we can have time to ourself (alone) afterward without any worry about the kind of relationship we are (not) developing with our child.

We can read stories about topics that *we* are interested in, and try to make it entertaining for the child. We can play games of skill, memory, sports, or intellect that keep our attention (even if we let her win). We can *make up* stories – you start it, and then you ask the child to continue it ("What do you think he did next?"), taking turns until the story is finished. We can tickle each other, play with the infant together, take the dog for a walk in the park, collect leaves, or throw stones in the lake. We can watch birds and look them up in our book, bring new friends to life through puppets, have a race, exercise, play hide-and-seek, or play games on the computer. We can go skating, tobogganing, or take on a park full of kids in soccer.

The possibilities are, truly, infinite. There are many things we can enjoy together if we make the effort and take the time. It does, however, require us to turn the TV off for a while, and get up off the sofa.

It pays off a hundredfold. You will look forward to that time together, guard it jealously. It will be a much-savored escape from the stresses of the day, and you will see your child change, progress, and develop in so many areas. You will notice the little things she does, and take joy in her new mastery, cuteness, or hugs. The child will look forward to your coming home at the end of a day, running out to jump in your arms when she hears footsteps or sees the car turn up the driveway. A good relationship with your child means so much . . . it just seems to make life more worthwhile. If it doesn't, then you're not enjoying your child; you're not getting from her what she has to offer.

There is little in this world that is more precious, more basic and innate, than to love and be loved by a child. But it does not come automatically. It is not gained simply by sowing that seed. A good relationship requires time together, attention, and having fun. It is not deserved, and will not come, just because we are his parents, because we put food on the table, a roof over his head, and a shirt on his back. It comes from touching, teaching, talking, praising, laughing, playing, and even discipline. This is what shows we really care. This is what makes us parents.

Rewards or bribes?

S ome people think that a reward is a bribe, unnatural, or it just
goes against the grain to offer a child a reward for doing
something: "After you get into bed, I'll bring you a cookie."

I share that concern . . . up to a point. It is well known that
children can get used to rewards, and come to expect them for
everything they do. It is always better not to use tangible, artificial rewards if we can help it.

On the other hand, however, at times there seems to be nothing else we can say or do to help. Sometimes the "natural" environment just isn't sufficient to get the job done. In such
situations, a tangible reward – artificial though it may be – may
still help. The fact is it is often quite effective. It spurs the child
on, gets him to do something he otherwise wouldn't do.
Moreover, he does it without a fight, without opposition – in
fact, quite happily, if we are offering a good reward.

The issue, then, is not *whether* to use rewards, but *when* to use
rewards. If the behavior is important, and if we cannot find
another way to encourage it, then there is nothing wrong with
using rewards. What's the alternative? Not to teach? Let the
child stay up until all hours? Moreover, if it is used properly, it
will have no ill-effects whatsoever.

My three-year-old son hated to go to the toilet to have a bowel
movement, even though he readily urinated in the toilet. He
would stand rigid, tense his rear end, and wait until the urgency
was gone. He didn't go for days on end, and then went in his
pants. He knew what was expected, and it didn't hurt him to go;
he simply hated doing it. No cajoling, encouragement, modelling, or praise could get him to go on that toilet. So, one day, a bit
worried about the situation, I offered him "a surprise" if he went
on the toilet. Hmmmm . . . he hesitated for a second, then asked,
"What is the surprise?" (I knew I had him.) I offered a new He-
Man character . . . and he flew up the stairs. Wow, I thought, this
is great . . . a lot of peace of mind for a few dollars. I was feeling
pretty full of myself until the next day, when he said, "If I go,
will I get a surprise?" Oh-oh, I knew it was too easy. Yet, I
wanted him to get used to using the toilet – let him master it, let

become a habit, let him experience the relief that comes along with it – before I removed the rewards. So, I bought four or five different He-Man characters, and gave one to him each day for several days, if of course he had a bowel movement in the toilet. Then, as it became easy and comfortable for him, I changed my tune a little: "We'll get one tomorrow, I don't have one right now." In short, he only got "paid" every second day, then every third day, and then it was dropped altogether (praise was, however, given lavishly when he used the toilet). He stopped asking for and expecting a "surprise," and he continued to use the toilet. There was not a single instance of soiling, or refusing to go since the first day we used a reward. The whole procedure took about two weeks (and cost me five or six toys), and then it was over. No muss, no fuss. It was . . . easy.

I didn't like the idea of "paying" him to go to the toilet one bit. But, I was worried about the situation. And I was therefore extremely pleased that it could be used, that it was so effective, that I had this "tool" at my disposal as a last resort because I simply could not find another way to get him to do it (without forcing him – causing wars, upsets, and making the whole toileting experience aversive to him). Most important, by praising him when he did go, and fading out the tangible rewards as it became a routine, I could easily and quickly remove (fade) those rewards.

Usually, such artificial rewards are not necessary. We should *not* get in the habit of "paying" a child in order to get him to do anything and everything (hug Auntie Jane, whom he may not like; say "please"; tidy up) because he may actually *become* noncompliant unless he is paid for his co-operation. Used sparingly, however, this is not a problem. We can and should use such rewards when nothing else (short of punishment) seems to work, when it is important to us or a real problem/difficulty for the child. It is a powerful way to motivate a child, a *temporary* measure, and often quite effective.

Give children a choice

Many times we can prevent oppositional behavior, tantrums, aggression, and the like, if we offer the child a choice. If it is cold outside, there is no question the child must wear a long-sleeved shirt. If we tell him, "Put on this shirt," he may object, delay, or refuse. Oftentimes, however, if we say, "Do you want to wear this shirt or that shirt?" there is no opposition, he has a choice. In a similar way, when it is time to do the marketing, we don't ask her if she wants to go, or drag her along, we ask her whether she wants to buy "Silly Crunch" cereal or "Snap, Crackle and Pop"; whether she wants to push the shopping cart or ride in it; whether she wants to buy the chocolate cookies or the Oreo cookies. When it's time to turn off the TV, we ask whether he wants to turn if off or if he wants me to turn it off, whether he wants to turn it off now or in two minutes, and so on.

It certainly does not prevent all opposition, but it does prevent a lot of it. Children like to be in control, they "want to do it myself." It can take the sting out of decisions that might otherwise cause problems.

Quality of life

Quality of Life . . . I'm not sure what it is, but I know everyone wants a whole bunch. It has something to do with freedom, dignity, having opportunities to learn or advance, having some fun. But it's hard to put your finger on; it's hard to count or measure on a ledger. Does my life, and my child's life, have "quality"? How can we get more? You don't have to know how to define it, or measure it, to get some more. In fact, you can add a bucketful.

The best way to understand what another person is going through is to go through it with them. So, I lived "a day-in-the-life" of some of my clients.

Barry, for example, was a two-year-old. He couldn't talk yet, or understand much of what was said to him. He also had little in the way of appropriate social or play skills, as is true for most two-year-olds. The family had many toys for him, but mostly they were hand-me-downs from his older brother. Barry actually had no way to fill his free time because he didn't really go for these toys, and the few he liked were well-worn by now.

Barry did some inappropriate things, too, like throwing toys, scratching, and hitting people.

Since Barry couldn't talk, I couldn't talk. If Barry was punished, I was punished. Everything done by or to Barry, was also done by or to me.

The day was eye-opening, to say the least. It quickly became clear that the most loving, caring, well-intentioned parents can still provide a very poor quality of life for their child. If one more person patted me on the head that day, I'd have cut their fingers off at the third knuckle. If one more person said, "Don't do that," I'd have thrown up. It also bothered me that we didn't have one minute of privacy in the whole day; we were watched, or at least in sight, at all times.

During the morning, his brother was busily stabbing Barry with a toy sword, and Barry swung at him. Mom only saw Barry's uppercut, so Barry (and I) were reprimanded. I almost had a conniption. Furthermore, we couldn't talk, so there was nothing we could do about the injustice. We did throw a toy, and hit ourselves, but mom didn't seem to understand that this was the only way to communicate, the only way to express that a wrong had been done, or perhaps it was just letting out some frustration. There was lots of free time, but we didn't know how to play with many of the toys, and we didn't like most of the others. So we sifted dirt.

There were so many people responsible for us during the day – mom, dad, relatives, a baby-sitter, daycare staff, a neighbor – that we felt like we didn't know any of them very well; we felt close to none, and were sure none of them felt very close to us.

That evening, I met with the parents to discuss Barry's quality of life. We decided to search for toys and leisure activities that were meaningful and enjoyable *to Barry*, rather than just using the "old" toys that his brother used to like (Barry definitely had different tastes). We decided to stay away from rote pats on the head and "good boy." We decided that fewer people would be

responsible for Barry during the day, so they could get to really
know and care about each other. We decided to spend more time
talking to Barry, showing him what words and gestures he could
use to express his needs and wants. And no reprimands were
permitted, unless the parents knew for sure what had preceded a
tantrum or disruptive act.

The message here is an important one, one that applies to
every child, every parent, every marriage. To understand the
pressures on mom, dad should be mom for a while. To understand the pressures on dad, mom should follow dad around for a
day. The parents can then gain more respect, even admiration,
for what the other does; they can then understand why the other
is occasionally frazzled, distracted, inattentive; they will be more
apt to do something constructive about it.

When we are worried about whether we are bringing up our
children properly; whether our spouse is doing his or her fair
share; whether we are treating our elderly (e.g. parents) with
dignity and humanity – we can try taking their place for awhile.
Perhaps we should continue to do this, on a regular basis,
making changes as we go, until we look forward to it, until it is
enjoyable to live a day in *their* life. Then we may all have a better
quality of life.

Teaching morals, ethics, and values

We all want our children to know the difference between
right and wrong, good versus bad. We want them to
value sincerity, thoughtfulness, honesty, helping others. But how
do we teach it? How do we instill in them a real feeling, a striving, for morals and ethics?

Instruction, by itself, has never been very effective. To simply
explain the difference between right and wrong is not enough. It
presumes that a child is already motivated to be ethical, and
needs only to learn how. This does not appear to be true; he also
must learn that it can feel good to do the "right" thing, to help
others, to be compassionate.

There are several ways to teach ethics, and in fact we use them
all the time. We may not realize we're doing it, but we are. If we

know some of the principles, perhaps we can then do it better, and rest a little easier.

When my son first labelled the letter "A," I told him, "That's right! Way to go! Boy are you smart!" I not only praised his efforts because I was pleased (and I wanted to encourage him further), but I *labelled* those efforts as "smart." In short, I was not only praising him, encouraging him to learn more, but I was *also* telling him that being smart is a "good" thing. After using the word a few times, he adopted it, used it spontaneously in other situations, and asked if "this" too was smart. I was teaching him values.

In the same way, one can talk about sharing, caring, helping, and so on. If we *encourage* such behaviors, *praise* them, and at the same time *label* them for the child, he comes to value those words and what they mean. He internalizes them and comes to really appreciate those qualities.

In a similar way, we can teach a child about the kinds of behavior that we don't like, by labelling them and pairing them instead with negative feedback, reprimands, etc. "William's mommy called to ask if we have his Transformer. Is this William's Transformer? You told me you found it on the street. When you don't tell me what really happened, it's called "lying," and lying is wrong. Now go to your room."

Oftentimes, we can do the same thing by commenting on other children's behavior. "Look what that boy did. He called that girl a bubble-head. That's mean; he made the girl sad. His mommy will be very mad at him." In this way, we can teach our children a lot about right and wrong by noticing the many examples of it in other children. The more examples our child sees, the better will be his understanding of what is "right" and "wrong." In the same way, we can teach a child the differences between being friendly and unfriendly, honest vs. dishonest, compassionate vs. uncaring, love vs. hate. While such concepts are complex, changing and taking shape over many years, they start (in their simplest forms) in childhood.

One of the most powerful tools for teaching ethics, morals, and values is of course modelling. Children tend to adopt many of the behavioral styles and patterns of parents. It would do no good to tell a child that swearing is bad, if our own speech is laced with swear words. A child won't know what's right or wrong if you tell him not to lie, and then he hears mommy tell someone on the phone that daddy is sick or not at home (when daddy is sitting right there and just didn't want to speak to the person). Children seem all too able to find those times when our own behavior violates our own edicts – and, while it may seem comical, beyond their understanding, or justified in your case, it will be confusing to a child. He too will make up his own "exceptions" to the rule, when it suits his needs.

A parent's behavior must be in line with that parent's edicts – if they're not, either the (parent's) behavior or the edicts must change, so the child can know what is right and what is wrong.

4

HOW PARENTS CAN HELP THEIR CHILD: SPECIFICS

Overview

Normal problems of normal children

Before discussing the individual behaviors that most concern parents, it is important to put them in proper perspective. It is crucial to understand that *all* children will exhibit *many* of these behaviors at some time during the first five to six years. Consequently, these are not abnormal; in fact, it would be rather surprising if they did not show up. We have all heard about "the terrible twos," "stranger anxiety" at around eight months of age, the "hyperactivity" that dominates many four-year-olds, the "NO" (oppositional) stage in children – these clearly show that normal development is fraught with many upsetting child behaviors. That's OK. That's part and parcel of being a child. What is of concern is whether they *continue* too long, and this chapter will specify for each behavior how long it should last, what is "too long," when it is and is not a real problem.

We will try to do several things in this chapter. We will describe the different kinds of child behaviors that are most often of some concern to parents, discuss why they occur, explain when they are and are not a problem, report on their incidence (i.e. how often they occur in other normal children), and of course describe the parenting procedures that are (and are not) often effective.

We will start with the early problems of infancy (i.e. crying, feeding, sleeping difficulties) and work up through the later problems of the four- to six-year-old (i.e. noncompliance, hyperactivity, aggression, speech problems), so the child behaviors that follow are listed in their approximate order of occurrence during child development.

If you are concerned about something your child does, you can rest assured that you are not alone. Table 4-1 shows how often other parents regard various kinds of behavior as problems in their own children. Fully 80 percent of all parents are concerned at some point about temper tantrums in their young child, and 60 percent are upset because their children are noncompliant. Two out of every three parents complain about sleeping difficulties – nightmares, trouble getting them to bed, waking up in the night, restless sleep, tantrums when the parent leaves the bedroom, etc. Almost half of all parents become concerned that their child is too active, "bouncing off the walls," always on the go, unable to sit still for even a few minutes. An incredible 43 percent of all parents are concerned about their child's fears, and this 43 percent only includes parents reporting multiple fears in their child. And the list goes on and on. Moreover, on average, a given child (boy or girl) will show five or six of these "problems" *at each age level*, beginning at 21 months through 11 years of age.

This list is not meant to scare you. Quite the contrary. It shows how common these are in *normal* development; it shows that these are normal developmental phases that most children pass through and grow out of. It should be comforting to know that the behavior you are concerned about does in fact occur in many, many children; it won't make you jump for joy, and it won't make you calm in the face of a tantrum or stuttering, but you'll be a bit less concerned, a bit less anxious about it and your child's future.

Many parents have this (unrealistic) view of an "ideal" child, an ideal that no child can possibly meet. So, as parents, we notice those deviations from the ideal, we worry about them, we become overly concerned about every little thing. This is in part why we find so many *parental* concerns about their child's behavior – they notice and worry about everything. So the numbers in Table 4-1 do not reflect the incidence of real problems in

---

Table 4-1

The frequency of mothers concerned about a problem in their own child:

Behavior	Percent of children
Temper tantrums	80
Sleeping problems – going to sleep, nightmares, waking up repeatedly during the night	68
Noncompliance	60
Hyperactivity	49
Fears	43
Toileting	43
Eating Difficulties	37
Restlessness	30
Thumbsucking	27
Biting, sucking, or chewing inappropriate objects	16
Picking sores	16
Grinding teeth	14
Unusual movements – jerking or twitching	12
Chewing or biting inside of mouth	11
Shyness	less than 10
Physical timidity	less than 10
Irritability	less than 10

---

children – far from it – they simply represent *parental* concerns, and parents are known to be overly sensitive and concerned. As we learn about child development, and watch our children grow, we eventually become more realistic and less concerned about the minor deviations from the "ideal" child.

We should also remember that while most children do engage in such upsetting behavior, they're actually doing it only a small proportion of the time. Most of the time we are captured by those adorable facial expressions; how wonderful it feels to make them laugh; how fulfilling it is to feel the child hug and kiss you;

how her face lights up with a smile when mommy or daddy comes into the room; not to mention our awe and wonder at what those big brown eyes are taking in, what she's really seeing and thinking.

One other note should be of some comfort. With few exceptions, these behaviors have not been found to lead to any maladjustment later in life. The fears, sleeping problems, irritability, toileting problems, self-injurious acts, which we see in childhood, do not mean that they will continue later on, nor are they associated with other problems of adjustment (social, work, school, emotional or intellectual functioning). Quite the contrary: they often decrease without any special intervention, with no known aftereffects. The two major exceptions to this are hyperactivity – which is particularly common in four-year-olds, but should disappear before the age of six and a half – and severely antisocial behavior (aggression, tantrums, noncompliance, and oppositional behaviors), which by the time it is "severe" is already a problem and should be dealt with immediately. Both of these, as we'll see, may grow and worsen, persisting through adolescence and later on, having a multitude of repercussions on school, friendships, family relations, and so on.

Infancy

Several of the following sections do not deal with infancy, for a couple of reasons. First, many of these behaviors, such as aggression, noncompliance, toilet training, social behavior, etc., are simply not present in, nor relevant to, infancy. Second, the majority of parental questions during infancy are concerned with possible medical problems, not behavioral problems, and medical problems are simply outside my area of expertise.

There are, however, some parental concerns about behavior during infancy that are the province of this book – crying, feeding, activity levels, sounds an infant should make, etc., and these are discussed in their appropriate sections.

Eating problems

The very first concern you will have about your child will probably be about feeding (after, of course, we find the baby is physically normal). It begins on day one, when we anxiously wait to see how the child will take to the breast or bottle. "Is she getting enough?" "Is he getting too much?" And, God forbid, "Why won't she take my breast?" Just try to console a mother whose baby won't take the breast the first instant it is presented – "She doesn't like me!" "There's something wrong with me!" "Oh God, whatam-Igonnado?!" Even though the nurse explains that this is common, that it can last one or two days, that there's no risk to the baby, and that it's often a simple matter of finding the right position for mom, baby, and breast, there is no way to console the mom who feels she has failed her first and most fundamental test of motherhood . . . until a few minutes (or hours) later when the right position is found and the proud momma can smile through her tears and delight in nurturing that baby.

A parent's first responsibility, and probably the purest form of dependency in a child, lies in feeding. No wonder we attach so much emotion, concern, and anxiety to feeding. This concern will continue through the years, although the specific issues may change. It will at times focus on the relative benefits of breast milk versus cow's milk (or formula); demand - versus schedule-feeding; the effects of food on activity level, health, vision, stools, and mood; whether a child is eating too much or not enough, is too fat or too thin; along with a concern for getting enough (but not too much) protein, vitamins, fats, etc. Our society is wracked with concern about food, diet, and appearance – is it any wonder then that we are concerned so early with how big or small our children are, with how much and what they eat.

While our early concern for feeding is a bit overdone, it is of course not without some merit. The literature shows that 80-85 percent of substantially overweight children continue to be substantially overweight as adolescents and adults. Volumes of literature show the health hazards, as well as psychological and social difficulties, due to extremes in weight.

Rarely is there any real problem with regard to eating during the first six years. Nonetheless, it is clear that our eating patterns and biology interact during this time to set a course for the future. So, our discussion here will focus on prevention because we do play a role in setting the occasion for subsequent problems, or else preventing such problems, during the early years. We'll begin with common parental concerns about eating in infancy, then turn to pica (eating inedible objects), overeating and undereating.

Parental concerns and norms during infancy

i. Eating patterns during the first year

The infant is equipped at birth with rooting and sucking reflexes. The rooting reflex is demonstrated when an object touches a child's cheek, and the baby turns his mouth toward it. We mention it here because it helps to understand a common error made in initial breast-feeding. Oftentimes, the mother or nurse places her hand on the baby's cheek to guide it toward the breast (or bottle), and of course the baby turns his head and mouth toward the hand rather than the breast. Hence, mom concludes the baby does not want the breast (and mom goes bananas). Instead, the breast should touch the baby's cheek.

The rooting reflex is strongest when the baby is hungry, and it is weak or absent when he is full. In addition, it may be dulled by sedatives given to the mother during delivery, which may last several days after delivery; this of course is one reason why it is quite common for infants not to take to the breast immediately.

The sucking reflex is universally present in newborns. Newborn infants suck on virtually anything placed in the mouth, and seem to enjoy sucking even when no food is obtained. The desire to suck remains strong for at least 12-15 months, sometimes as long as two to three years, as the baby alternates between the breast, the bottle, fingers, and pacifiers.

Hunger and appetite are weak during the first seven to ten days, and hunger demands are irregular. By two to three weeks of age, the infant is getting hungry more often, and by four weeks it becomes quite regular, with feedings about every three hours or so. Appetite is especially strong between four and twelve weeks; the infant often takes in more than his body can handle, and frequent regurgitation is common at this age. Thereafter, hunger continues to become more regular until about one year of age, when appetite falls off. In general, the first year is characterized by rapid growth and a healthy (regular) appetite, as babies normally triple their birth weight by their first birthday.

Food preferences may appear early; after all, taste buds are fully developed at birth. During the latter half of the first year, cereal is often the preferred cuisine, although different kinds may be demanded (oatmeal is a common favorite). During the second year, the appetite becomes much more discriminating (i.e. pickier), and strong likes and dislikes become evident.

ii. Breast- versus bottle-feeding

Most research suggests that breast milk is the preferred food for infants. Breast-fed babies are less prone to stomach upsets. Breast-feeding also provides greater immunity to infection as well as fewer channels for infection.

Still, the advantages of breast-feeding to a baby are not really that great. One illustrative study found that 37 percent of bottle-fed babies suffered from respiratory infection, while 28 percent of breast-fed babies suffered the same – a difference, but not a terribly large one, as infections are common in infants during the first year. Also, all of these infections were in fact handled rather early and easily by the physician and mother, with no further or lasting repercussions to the baby.

While breast-feeding is a source of satisfaction and comfort for some mothers, it is somewhat troublesome to others: the milk may leak between feedings (despite the use of padding), drenching clothes or bedding; it ties the mother up frequently and for lengthy periods of time; fathers may get jealous or object because they want to participate in the feeding of their babies; the breasts can ache, swell, get bitten or gummed to death; the working mother may not be available to breast-feed (or worse, may feel that "mothering" comes in conflict with "career").

In general, breast-feeding is slightly better for infants than bottle-feeding – *not* because it is "natural" (earthquakes are natural, too), but because it seems to provide more immunity to infection. Nonetheless, the advantages are not overwhelming, and they continue to be reduced as formulas improve. Consequently, the deciding factor will probably be an emotional one for most families – if a mother enjoys the breast-feeding, or otherwise feels it important, then she will do it; on the other hand, if it is not that big of an issue, mom works, dad wants to feed the baby too, or it just ties mom down too much and too often, she may not breast-feed. Many families, however, find that a combination of breast- and bottle-feeding is the most convenient and enjoyable approach. Mom can breast-feed when it is convenient to do so; breast milk can be put in a bottle for dad to feed the baby; formula can be used when time is short.

Either way, there is no reason for guilt or self-recrimination. Millions of babies are adopted each year, many mothers cannot (medically) breast-feed for one reason or another, and these children appear to grow up just as healthy, happy, adjusted (or delinquent) as breast-fed babies. And do not let anyone tell you that attachment or bonding is somehow reduced if you do not breast-feed – such emotional bonding comes if one often holds a baby, rocks her, sings to her, loves her, dotes over her, and cares for her . . . and this cannot come out of a breast. It is the love and tenderness that is important, not the breast, and if breast-feeding unduly inconveniences a mother (or family), it can actually *interfere* with that loving and that tenderness.

iii. Some "tricks" for introducing the breast
Many babies do not take to the breast right away. In one study, 40 percent of newborns had to be actively assisted before they would suck on the breast. The child may be tired and uninterested when it is offered; the child's hunger may be dulled for several days by the anesthetic given to mom during labor; the child may have some difficulty getting or keeping the nipple in his mouth; it may take awhile to find a position comfortable for both of you; and hunger is known to be weakest, and quite variable, during the first seven to ten days. So, if your baby has some trouble nursing at first, relax; it's quite common.

There are some things you can do, however, to help the baby

along. *First*, of course, mom should look for a comfortable position for nursing. The sitting position seems to be most popular among mothers (although it can be done lying down or standing up). Try sitting up in bed with big pillows behind your back and head for support. Put a pillow on your lap, and the baby on the pillow. Bring (bend) your knees up, to bring the baby closer, and bend forward (scrunch up the pillow behind you for support) to make the breast closer and more accessible to the baby. Once you have nursed the baby a few times, and relaxed, you will find your favorite position and place (i.e. a favorite chair) for nursing.

Second, take advantage of the rooting reflex. Touch the nipple to the corner of the mouth, or brush his cheek with it, until he turns his mouth toward the nipple. When he opens his mouth, gently bring him closer to the nipple. Do not use the hand to touch the baby's cheek, as the child will turn toward the hand instead of the nipple.

Third, it can be frustrating for the infant until he learns that he must take the whole areola (the dark circle around the nipple) into his mouth, not just the nipple. Mom can help by slowly and lightly brushing the nipple up and down against the upper and lower lip, "teasing" the child, until he opens his mouth wider (wide enough to take both the nipple and the areola). Also, you can pinch the breast with your fingers, above and below the areola, to help the child focus on the "correct" portion of the breast.

Fourth, mom can squeeze a little milk out of the breast, and brush the breast and these drops of milk against the child's lips. The taste of the milk will increase the child's interest and motivation, and he will of course focus on the breast because that's where the "taste" came from.

Fifth, a common frustration for newborns during breast-feeding is that they can't breathe because their nose gets buried in the breast. You can press your finger on top of your breast to keep it away from the baby's nose, or bring her legs closer to you so that her body will naturally be at an angle that keeps her nose free.

Finally, sometimes the child can't take the breast into his mouth because the breast is too full and hard. Mom should check this and if necessary remove some of the milk before feeding the baby.

iv. Weaning from the breast

In North America, it is customary to wean a baby off the breast between six and eight months. Weaning earlier usually presents no difficulties for the baby; weaning later, however, during the second six months of life, may cause some problems, such as refusal to eat, loss of weight, and dehydration.

The best way to prevent such problems is to *substitute a bottle for one of the daily feedings sometime during the first four months* – it does not have to be rigidly scheduled, but done with some regularity just to get the baby used to the bottle. Most recommend that you start this before the child is two months old, if you plan to use a bottle. If you do get the baby accustomed to the bottle early, then there should be no problem whenever you decide to wean the child completely from the breast. This can be done easily and gradually by replacing one meal at a time with the bottle or solid food.

If the infant does not take to the bottle right away, first try different nipples. Many children dislike one shape, but suck quite contentedly on another. In addition, check the opening to see if the flow of milk is too fast or too slow. This is especially true for breast-fed babies because the infant must suck a good deal harder on the breast (than on the bottle) to get milk, and this strong sucking may at first bring more milk from a bottle than the baby expected. If the hole is too small, the child may get frustrated, agitated, and of course cry because he is still hungry. If the infant refuses the bottle, but takes pudding or baby food well, it is possible to give an adequate amount of milk by spoon or cup, or by cooking cereals or pudding in milk. Alternatively, you can put breast milk in the bottle to help the baby adapt to bottle-feeding. In infants over nine months, it may be helpful to let the child hold the bottle or cup.

v. Demand - versus schedule-feeding

Parents who feed their baby on demand will find that the baby develops a schedule anyway. However, that schedule may start at 8:00 a.m. one day, and 5:00 a.m. another. It can be difficult to run a household, or hold a job, with a routine that changes unpredictably each day.

At one month of age, most babies will adjust to a four-hour schedule which starts at the same time each day; and since this is convenient in many homes, many parents adopt it. One should keep in mind, however, that some babies will be unhappy with this interval, perhaps needing more frequent and smaller meals for a time, and parents must be prepared to accommodate and change when necessary.

Another aspect of demand - versus schedule-feeding concerns how much the baby eats. Most researchers suggest that we should let them eat as much as they want. Babies on the breast may vary widely at different feedings, sometimes taking eight ounces, sometimes only two ounces. Whether using a breast or a bottle, one should not try to force or restrict the baby – his appetite will vary and this is quite normal. If there are any extremes – a sudden decrease in milk consumption, skipping several consecutive feedings, consistently taking in only two ounces, wanting to be fed every two hours – then you should consult your physician.

The infant typically drops the night (i.e. 2:00 a.m.) feeding anywhere between three weeks and three months of age, and then the evening feeding (i.e. 10:00 p.m.) is omitted shortly thereafter (one to two months later). A three-meal-a-day schedule can often be introduced at five to eight months – depending of course on the child's appetite, sleeping habits, and acceptance of solid foods – with bottles used to supplement the meals as needed.

vi. Solid foods
In the first few months, an infant will push his tongue out against any solid foods. By three to four months, however, a change occurs – the tongue now tosses food to the back of the mouth. Consequently, this is an optimal time to introduce the first taste of "solid" (mushy) foods. Puréed vegetables and meats are often used first, followed later by cereal, cottage cheese, mashed banana and other fruits, yogurt, any of the commercial

strained baby foods, and, of course, almost anything that can be put in a blender and comes out mushy. Many recommend introducing solids at the evening meal, when babies are often more playful, sociable, and prone to experiment. Once the first mushy food is accepted, then virtually any mushy foods are acceptable to use (although most now recommend that puréed vegetables and meats should be used first, and fruits last, since fruits are more apt to cause minor stomach irritations).

Soft foods that require chewing can be introduced as early as seven to nine months, even though no teeth are present – the infant will gum and gnaw it to death, and it's good practice for chewing. (For example, most children like to gnaw on pizza crust, after it has been baked or microwaved until it is hard.)

One word of warning – when that good mush is accepted, many babies don't accept the bottle as readily or as often as they once did. The solid food tastes better *and* it's fun to play with: a child can spread it out, rub it on his face and in his hair, run his fingers through it, hit the bowl and watch the food fly, and throw in on the floor – what can you do with milk or the bottle? Be ready to give up the bottle (except at naps and bedtime), and you'll have to "prepare" each meal.

Pica (eating things that aren't food)

Normal children under the age of nine to ten months put virtually everything into their mouths that will fit in there. From ten months up to four years of age, they no longer put *everything* into their mouths, but they aren't very discriminating about what does go in there. Acorns, nails, paint, cigarette butts, medicine capsules, and all kinds of unrecognizable and reprehensible things found only underneath sofas, deep in the carpet, or stuck to the floor are all fair game. This, too, is normal – not to say permissible – and the proper "treatment" is parental supervision combined with "child-proofing" the house.

After four years of age, however, the child should no longer be doing this. After four years of age, the developmental phase has passed, and it must be stopped: the dangers are too great, ranging from poisoning to damaging internal organs. Professional consultation will be needed and, unless there is a medical cause, a form of punishment may well be a part of treatment.

Undereating

i. Normal patterns of undereating
Children go through tremendous swings in appetite during normal development. Hunger is low and irregular during the first seven to ten days of life, and it may scare you. In fact, a newborn may lose up to 10 percent of his weight in the first week or two. Then hunger starts to take hold with zest, as the child triples his birth-weight in the first year (with some plateaus here and there, but they don't last too long). The period between one and five years, however, is one of slow growth, as the average weight gain is only about five pounds per year. Moreover, weight gain is often quite irregular during this time, as months pass without any gain whatsoever. As the gain in weight slows, the child needs less food and the appetite is reduced. Parents often become concerned during this time because the child often just isn't hungry and seems content to miss several meals for a while.

Our emotions and anxieties about feeding may resurface with a vengeance during this time, as something is scary about not being able to feed our child – something seems fundamentally wrong with the child if he doesn't seem interested in eating.

Nothing is wrong. The body needs less because it is growing more slowly, and the growth is occurring in fits and spurts. As long as the child does get hungry at least once per day, and eats well during that meal, there is nothing to worry about. If your child eats less often, looks pale and drawn, or you are otherwise concerned, then a chat with your physician will usually be helpful and reassuring.

Coercion and nagging are unnecessary and ineffective. The only time I would really try to get my child to eat is if I knew that he'd be hungry if he would just stop playing long enough to notice. It is true that children love to play, and usually hate to do anything – including eating – if it interferes with play. Sometimes, we know that our child gets irritable, unmanageable, and "bounces off the walls" if he doesn't eat something for lunch. If so, we can simply forewarn him ("It'll be time to eat in five minutes."), then serve the food, and then take away the toys if necessary until he's had something to eat.

ii. When it is a problem, and what to do

It is very rare indeed for a child under six years of age to be "anorexic" – that is, to reject food to the point where it is physically unhealthy and unsafe. The anorexic child is *not* a picky eater – he is a *non*-eater. If a child is fussy about food, or eats one day but not the next, it shows he *does* like (some) foods. It is when a child indiscriminantly rejects all foods, and consistently does this (to the point of losing weight), that we may consider the problem of anorexia.

The "popular" and common use of the term anorexia refers to an actual *fear* of food, anxiety about eating, and extreme concern for body-image. To my knowledge such extreme fear of food has never been reported in young children – it begins typically in adolescence. In those few cases where anorexia does occur in children, it is usually caused by a disease of some type, not by fear, and a physician should be consulted. It will usually start rather abruptly, and be associated with weight loss, apathy, listlessness, tiring easily – and it is most often quite obvious and easy to detect. It is, however, exceedingly rare in children under six years of age.

While we rarely have to worry about anorexia in children, there are strategies that may help improve a child's appetite and make mealtimes more enjoyable. If a child dislikes a food, we may substitute another in order to make eating a more enjoyable experience. The atmosphere and surroundings at mealtime should be pleasant. The food should be prepared to the child's liking, and the child may be given a choice of foods. Small portions should be used, and the child should not be required to eat everything put on his plate. And parents should not discuss the foods they dislike in front of the child.

Overeating

Approximately one of five adults are substantially overweight, almost twice as many women as men. It is considered the number one health hazard in North America, bar none. And it usually starts in childhood.

A growing body of research shows that a person's weight is *not* simply a function of the calories eaten. There's a good deal more to it, and understanding what causes weight gain may help us to control weight in children, without stress or deprivation (diets).

i. Causes of weight gain

There are several factors that contribute to weight: heredity, physiology, activity level, and eating habits.

Heredity gives us our size and physical constitution, as well as a beginning number of fat cells. Our physiology determines how quickly we process and use ("metabolize") calories. Activity level determines how many of these calories we use up (rather than storing them as fat). And eating habits determine what we eat, how much, why, and when – in short, how many calories we take in.

Once fat cells are established, they can never be lost – they can only be reduced in size. We all have fat cells (they are normal), but fat people have more or larger fat cells.

In children, we find that overeating not only increases the size of fat cells, but also the *number* of fat cells. The *number* of fat cells is pretty much established for life by the time children reach 12 years of age (sometimes earlier), so it is much more difficult to lose (or gain) large amounts of weight after the age of 12: eighty percent of overweight children become overweight adults, and only a small percent of normal-size children become overweight later as adults. Clearly, childhood is a very critical time to establish proper eating patterns and body proportions.

Many parents mistakenly think that activity level is not that important because exercise is thought to consume little energy, and besides appetite increases when activity levels are high. In fact, the literature suggests that overweight children (six- to eight-year-olds) often have a drastically lower activity level than normal-size children; this is actually more common than their eating abnormally large amounts of food. Moreover, decreasing activity levels, even substantially, did *not* decrease the amount of food taken in.

Of course, it quickly becomes a vicious cycle as the burden of excess weight may further discourage activity. In addition, soon there are social and psychological problems if a child becomes obese – he often views himself as ugly, socially inadequate and undesirable as a friend.

Finally, it should be noted that very few children become fat unless at least one of the parents is fat. (You know what's coming, don't you?) While only 10 percent of children of normal-size parents become obese, it goes up to 50 percent if one parent is fat, and up to 80 percent if both parents are fat. It's unclear whether this is a function of genetics, or the poor eating habits and exercise levels of the parents, but one thing is clear – the overweight parent will have to change his or her eating habits in order to ensure the child is not excessively heavy. After all, modelling plays a major role in children's eating (and exercise) habits, just as it does in their learning of speech and social skills.

ii. When is it a problem?

A parent should not be overly concerned about a child's weight until at least the age of four or five. Many babies with lots and lots of "baby fat" turn out to be slim by the age of three or four; and I know many very slight children who achieved normal weight by the age of four – in many cases it is a pleasant and "astounding" change in body shape to the parents.

Research suggests that severe childhood weight problems usually begin between the ages of five to seven years, and this is when the number of fat cells may begin to increase most dramatically. It is at this age that we'll begin to keep an eye on body weight. Still, we must be careful about reading the weight charts – there is always a *range* of weight that is considered normal, and even this can vary according to a child's constitution (i.e. is he "big-boned"?). The charts are a guideline, and we should not be overly conscious of a single number or a precise "normal" body weight.

In general, if a child at this age or older is more than 20 percent above the expected norm for his height and age, then a parent should deal with it. Moreover, it will be quite obvious to you that there is a problem in weight because you will notice a lower activity level, an avoidance of peers, the names that other children may call him, etc.

I should emphasize that *we don't have to wait until there are weight problems – good eating and exercise habits are preventative (and never punitive if done properly), and equally applicable to children of normal weight. The strategies we will describe are appropriate for all children who are at least five years of age.*

Finally, we have noted that it is rare to become fat after the age of 12 (unless you were overweight earlier), so parents can feel quite proud if they have kept their child within the normal weight range for those seven years – ages five through 12. We've done our job and the child will probably never be a fat person.

iii. What not to do if your child is overweight

First, let's cover a few "Do nots," as these are common (yet ineffective) strategies that many parents use to control a child's weight:

1. We must never let a young child go hungry; there's simply no need.
2. We do not make a moral issue out of it – shaming her, blaming him, talking about the child or food as "good" or "bad," regarding the child as unsightly, ridiculous, or self-indulgent.
3. We do not expect children to do things we won't do, and we can't expect them not to eat things that we are eating.
4. Do not become overzealous – it's a matter of changing habits, which should be done with as little fuss as possible, not as a fanatic.
5. The use of drugs or appetite suppressants should not even be considered at this age unless there is a medical problem associated with weight gain (and it is closely monitored by a physician).
6. Finally, sermonizing is neither proper nor effective, and it tends to shift the entire responsibility to the child (where it does not belong).

iv. Preventing and handling excess weight gain in children

In many ways it is easier to tackle eating (and exercise) habits in children, as opposed to adults, because we simply have more influence over them. We control what foods are bought, what snacks are given, how much is put on the plate – and of course such controls go out the window when they become adults (or even at adolescence). In other ways, it's tougher to change children's eating patterns because in all probability *several* people must change their ways – the parents as well as the child – so we've got several "willpowers" and habits to contend with, not just one. It is for this reason that most children who fail or drop out of weight programs are the ones with overweight parents – the parents can't handle the normal eating and exercise patterns.

First, parents must understand that a child's weight must be kept in check during the early years, to prevent fatness later on. If weight can be held in check, the increase in the number of fat cells can be controlled. (As an aside, if you're curious, a normal child has about three billion fat cells, while an obese child often has six billion or more, and of course these are never lost later in life no matter how much reducing or exercise you do.)

Second, many parents have to get past the notion that a fat child is a healthy child. In many families, and in many cultures, children are encouraged to finish what's on their plate. Moreover, it is with special pleasure that we egg a child on to seconds – "Want some more spaghetti, honey? How about dessert?" What's more, we may even show some concern if they don't stuff themselves to the gills – "What's the matter, don't you like mommy's spaghetti?" – which of course the child picks up on. It becomes "expected" to not only eat everything dished out, but to ask for seconds. A child who goes on for seconds (and thirds) holds a special place, of course, in his mother's heart.

The dinner table is not the place for us to decide that we are good parents, at least not based on how much of our cooking is devoured. A fat child is *not* a healthy child – he is unhealthy, and the stage is being set for physical and social problems, not to mention a reduced life expectancy.

Third, we must deal with "snacks." There is nothing wrong with snacks for children. The issue is, however, what they should snack on. When I was growing up, a snack meant the "good stuff" – potato chips, peanut butter, apple pie, ice cream, cake and cookies, leftovers (especially old pizza). That's what a snack was, plain and simple. It wasn't until much later that I found out that people actually eat fruit, cheese, and other healthy things for a snack. But my wife recognized the problem, and to my utter shock and amazement, our kids not only snack on apples, cheese, grapes, nuts, raisins, etc., but they actually like them. Parents should set the patterns early, stay away from sweets, give them all the fruits, cheese, juice, etc. they want. Keep potato chips (barbecued, cheese-flavored, or otherwise), ice cream, chocolate cakes, out of the house – or save them for special occasions. If you must have them in the house (that is, the parents can't live without them), then get the child used to limited quantities – i.e. *one* cookie per day.

This is *not* to say we should become fanatics about it. We won't make an issue out of a child eating sweets at a birthday party or some other special occasion. Rather, we want to develop habits, daily routines that minimize sweets, so that they are exceptions rather than the norm.

Fourth, have one place to eat (and not in front of the TV). The child can eat all he wants, but it must be "at the table." In this way eating will cause a disruption in play, outdoor activities, and TV-watching. It will *compete* with other things the child likes to do, rather than allowing the child to do both at the same time. We are not born eating in front of the TV, and we should not start doing it – it will become a habit, and watching TV will come to mean we go get something to eat. This of course means that parents can't do it either – the child will see this and want to do it, too.

Fifth, overweight people often eat when they're happy, when they're sad, when good things happen (to "celebrate"), when they're stressed, and so on. Eating appears to be a soothing influence, something good we can give ourselves as a reward, or to counteract feeling low or upset. We not only model that for our child – and she picks it up and does the same – but we assume eating will help everyone else through the tough times. So, we offer the child food when she's disappointed, a favorite piece of cake if she goes to bed quietly, some ice cream to soothe her if a friend pushed her or called her names. Food should be offered at regular times (i.e. at normal meal- and snack-times) or when you think the child is really hungry. It should *never* be offered on the basis of mood, or as a soothing agent. Such habits, once developed, are very hard to break.

Sixth, we eat slowly, leisurely, at a moderate pace, and ask the child to do the same, if he gulps his food too quickly. It takes time for the physiological signals to go from the stomach to the brain, telling you that you're full. If you eat too fast, you will have overeaten by the time your brain tells you your stomach is packed. Hunger is signalled by muscle contractions in the stomach. As we eat, the "hunger" subsides as the contractions subside. The contractions do not subside as soon as the food goes into the mouth – the food has to be digested and, a few minutes later, it will affect the hunger. Eating at a moderate pace allows the stomach and brain to keep pace with how much you've eaten, and how full you're getting.

Seventh, don't shop for food when you're hungry, shop when you're full, especially if your child goes with you. When you're both full, you're not so tempted by all the "extra" sweet, salty, and fatty foods that we crave when we're hungry.

Eighth, make a list *before* you go to do the marketing, and buy *only* what's on that list.

Ninth, ensure that your child gets some exercise every day. With most children this is not a problem, since playing with friends or going to the preschool/kindergarten will take care of it. But overweight children may not participate, or may tire easily. If so, and you should check to find out, then we parents must supplement it. We can go for evening walks each day after work or after dinner, we can go to the park with a ball or frisbee and play with our child, we can stroll through a mall, go window-shopping, or put up a basketball hoop and shoot baskets together. We can go "exploring" in the park, visit animals at the zoo, go on nature walks, go looking for different kinds of birds, flowers, leaves, rocks, shells, etc. We can take the dog for a walk, go visit another child, and on and on.

It's really not hard to find ways to exercise each day, to find activities that both the parent and the child will enjoy. The problem here is rarely with the child. The problem, if we're honest, is getting the parents up off the sofa or away from their TV, computer, or dishes. The key to "exercise" is to do something that is fun. I'm not saying you must jog, walk two miles, or go to the gym (unless you enjoy it). Exercise simply will not be maintained (by the parents) if it is a struggle, a battle each day. Rather, if we do something fun – whether it's a walk along the lake, in the park, or gathering all the neighborhood kids to play soccer against us – then *we* will look forward to it.

Whether it's sports, walks, playing with animals (i.e. at the zoo), swimming, climbing, racing to the end of the street, rides, dancing, role-playing pet stories of knights and princesses, riding bicycles, just letting your child loose and following him around, or playing tag, there are many activities just waiting for us if we take a minute to think about them. Make the effort to call and find out where the public pool is, for example, and what times it is open. If it's fun, you'll not only keep it up, but you'll look forward to it.

A final, important point about exercise. Don't force your child if he's tired. When you first start this, the overweight child may tire easily. When he's tired, that's enough. As time goes by, his stamina will improve and he'll last longer. This happens naturally, if you do it most days. It *must* remain fun, or it is doomed (in fact it will become negative), so don't force a child to do more when he's tired.

Tenth, finally, is mealtime. Minimize fast foods (McDonald's, pizza, etc.) to the extent that it is practical and possible. Prepare basic foods (chicken, roast beef, etc.) in a tasty way, so that it is not just pizza, tacos, and greasy hamburgers that are "special" and taste good. Just like exercise, the key here will be to make "ordinary" foods taste good, so the child actually likes eating healthy foods. There are umpteen books of delicious recipes for calorie-counting people – it's a little extra work, a little extra preparation, but there are some recipes there for you and your child. This is *not* to say we're going on a diet – it's to say we're going to get in the *habit* of eating good foods, making lower calorie food more appetizing. Going hungry is not the answer – that's a struggle of will, and most of us eventually lose that struggle.

During mealtimes, we also serve smaller portions, and let the child have more (as much as she wants). Everyone tends to "clean their plate," so smaller portions will satisfy that tendency and the child will eat more (seconds) only if she's really hungry.

During each meal, serve the food that is *least* attractive (tasty) to the child first, when she is the hungriest. If you serve all the food together, she will eat her favorites first, and leave the rest. Oftentimes we can get a child to eat the less preferred food if it is served first, by itself, and then follow with the tastier portions.

Crying and tantrums

Crying is literally wired in (genetic) to children. For good reason. After all, parents are wired to react to crying – we jump, fast and high, when we hear our baby cry. It tells us when there is something wrong, and then we can help.

Responding to a baby's cry seems so basic to us, to our love for that child, and so fundamental to parenting, that it is awfully hard to resist. There comes a time, however, when we must. There comes a time when our child will cry not because he is in need, but rather because he wants 37 toys at the toy store, spaghetti instead of hot dogs, for you to play when you have to work, to watch "The Attack of the Mushroom People" on TV when you know it is too violent, and that it will scare him and cause nightmares.

The time to ignore crying will come for every parent, and it can be a gut-wrenching experience. Steel yourself. To sit in another room and listen to a child cry himself to sleep, when you know he just wants to sleep with you or hold your hand until he nods off, will try the will of the sturdiest of parents. Crying always got mommy or daddy to come before; why not now? So, the child then adds a little extra to her crying, for emphasis, to make sure you hear, to drive you up the wall – she'll start to yell, plead, stomp, and throw things. This, of course, is your basic tantrum. It seems to be an outgrowth or extension of crying.

If you fail to resist, if you put off that test too long, crying and tantrums will grow until the child is running every minute of your day. No wonder that studies have found 80 percent of parents to be concerned about tantrums and crying.

Definition and incidence
In newborns, crying can occur anywhere from about one to four hours per day. It steadily increases during the first six weeks of life, and six to eight weeks is the peak age of crying. But this crying is adaptive. A newborn cries when he is hungry, wet, soiled, startled, in an uncomfortable position, etc., and he will cry about 12 times per day on average (though this can vary widely among children). When a newborn cries, we (should) jump. We should not ignore crying for at least the first year. The more we hold the infant and generally care for her, the less crying she will do; studies reveal that holding a baby a minimum of four hours each day will reduce crying almost in half.

Over time, crying decreases. Just two to three months after birth, crying episodes are down to about four times per day. After one year of age, a child cries less about physical discomfort and more for environmental reasons – handling by strangers, at bedtime; crying for a preferred kind of food (rather than hunger, per se); wanting to be held constantly, etc. By age six, only 18 percent of children cry as much as two to three times per week.

As crying decreases, tantrums begin to appear, even as early as eight months of age. While crying is at times appropriate and valuable to us – when a child is hurt, afraid, or otherwise in need – tantrums are not. Tantrums are manipulative. And it seems that tantrums first appear as an added attraction to crying, when crying alone doesn't work. The child begins to scream instead of cry, tense her body, hold her breath, kick her legs and flail her arms. This soon grows into throwing things, foot-stomping, door-slamming, falling on the floor, hitting, kicking, and so on.

A tantrum is by definition manipulative; it is a child's attempt to get his way. All children will do it, although it may take many different forms in different children. It is perfectly normal, very common, and not at all deviant for tantrums to occur. After all, in the first year we jumped at every little squeak, and we even jumped in anticipation of a possible squeak. We jumped at "maybe squeaks" ("Honey, did you hear something?"), and we jumped at squeaks that were never squeaked (many new parents hear and see things that don't exist for several months). That's OK. Parents are part caterer, part concierge the first year: it's breakfast in bed, servants-in-waiting, the red carpet and a honeymoon, all rolled into one. But the child gets rather used to the royal treatment, having every whim met before it is even whimmed. How would you feel if the maid all of a sudden didn't answer the bell (cry)? You'd ring louder. Then you might yell. Who's the master and who's the slave around here anyway?

At some time, the child must learn that slavery has been abolished, that the bell won't work, that he can't have everything he wants. The longer you put it off, the more used to it he will become and the more difficult (and upsetting, for both of you) it will be to teach.

When are crying and tantrums a problem?
It is absolutely normal for crying and tantrums to occur. Such behavior is neither abnormal nor a problem – it is to be expected. The key is that it should decrease over time.

Tantrums become a problem, then, if they do not decrease, if they last too long. If a parent continues to serve a child, if tantrums are effective in a child getting his way, they will continue, increase, and become a dominant and pervasive pattern for interacting with other people (peers, teachers, siblings, parents, even strangers). Then, of course, it is a real problem, often leading to noncompliance, aggression, and difficulties at school. Moreover, as long as this behavior is dominant, the child will learn little if anything about appropriate social interactions, like sharing, turn-taking, compromising, co-operating, appropriate verbal requests (i.e. asking), and so on.

In short, we cannot prevent tantrums, but how we react to them will determine whether or not they continue. So, it is valuable to know how to handle tantrums *before* they become a serious problem.

How to handle crying and tantrums

For about the first year, I would not worry about crying – we should simply go to the child when she is upset. Later, we must distinguish between crying that is for a real need and crying that is manipulative. Most parents can distinguish these at some point, sometimes as early as six to eight months and sometimes not until the child is 12-15 months old. If you are not sure, simply check the child to see if she needs anything, and do not be too concerned about "making a mistake" in your handling of it during this early period.

When crying is clearly manipulative, or the child is otherwise tantrumous, there are several things we can do to make sure it does not continue too long:

1. *We make sure that a tantrum does not serve to get his way*

    This means of course that it is crucial to know what a child is tantrumming for. If you know that a child wants something – a TV show, candy, to go to the playground, to be picked up – then ignoring the child is effective. Ignoring him ensures that he doesn't get what he wants; the tantrum doesn't work. On the other hand, if he is trying to *avoid* something – tidying up his toys, going to bed, eating with a fork (instead of bending over and sucking the plate clean) – ignoring him is the worst thing we can do; if we ignore him, then he doesn't have to tidy up, go to bed, or use the fork, and the tantrum is successful (it got you to ignore him, and he got to do what he wanted). In this case, we treat it like noncompliance (see discussion on noncompliance, pages 118-127); we follow-through, by taking him to bed, holding the fork in his hand, or physically guiding him to tidy up.

    Do not listen to anyone who says you should always ignore a child when he throws a tantrum – this is a very common suggestion, even by professionals, in textbooks, and from child-rearing experts. Recent research clearly shows that this is a mistake, often counterproductive, and it will tell a child that tantrums *do sometimes* work. In any situation where a child is throwing a tantrum to avoid something (i.e. going to bed), to get out of something (i.e. going to school), or to resist your instructions (i.e. putting on a jacket), we must go to the child and follow through (put him to bed, take him to school, put on his jacket). To sit and wait for the child to stop throwing a tantrum, to leave the room, or to otherwise ignore him, would in fact delay going to school, going to bed, putting on the jacket – a hefty reward for his tantrum.

2. *Eliminate explanations and discussions during a tantrum*
During a tantrum, we shouldn't explain or discuss why he can't have candy now, why he can't have every toy he sees in the toy store. Virtually all young children love such attention and personal contact with parents. We don't want him to think that he can get it by throwing a tantrum because, the tantrum will increase simply to get our attention. We can explain why going to bed is important, why he can't have cookies before dinner, *at other times, before* a tantrum occurs. (Note: If a child asks nicely, we *can* discuss and explain why he can't have these toys; it is only when a tantrum occurs that we will eliminate or postpone such discussion.)

3. *These procedures must be used consistently*
It would be quite harmful if one parent catered to a child's tantrums while the other ignored him. The child will quickly learn who the tantrums will work with, instead of learning that they don't work at all. Similarly, we can't cave in half the time because we're too tired or too busy to face a scene. If we're too tired, upset, or preoccupied to deal with a tantrum, then we just give him the cookie when he first asks for it (*before* a tantrum occurs, so tantrums are not the way to get the cookie), or we ask our spouse to help us and deal with it this time.

4. *We teach a child appropriate ways to get what he wants*
We must show children how and when to share, take turns, and co-operate – they're not born with these skills.

If he wants a toy that another child is playing with, we help him to pick out an attractive toy to offer in exchange, we teach him to wait his turn, and we teach him to play together with the other child and share the toy. We try to do this in many different situations in which a child may be frustrated or denied something he wants ("Say, please"; "If you let Adam play with your bike, maybe he will let you play with his soccer ball"; "If you give Greta one of your cookies, she will be so-o-o happy"; "If you put on your pajamas all by yourself, daddy will be so proud of you."). We *never* just try to eliminate behavior, even tantrums; we must always establish, shape, and encourage alternative appropriate behavior to take its place.

5. *We look for the good things that children do, and praise them*
Dealing with tantrums can be trying at the beginning. The first few times you resist the tantrum, the child may go through a whole new repertoire in trying to figure a way to get what he wants, and it can last anywhere from 30 seconds to 30 minutes (or longer). We don't want such upsets to dominate the scene, or our relationship with the child. So we make a special effort, at other times, to look for the nice things that he does. And we praise them warmly. We can also play with him a bit more, talk to him, do some extra things together. In this way, the child learns that he is not a bad person, we do love him; it was just that behavior that we didn't like. By showing him the kinds of behavior we do like, and by having fun together, we can rest assured that there will be no damage to our relationship, or to the child's psyche, and confidently carry through with the procedures for dealing with tantrums.

6. *While we are trying to deal with tantrums, we do not take on any other major behaviors*
If tantrums occur on average once per day or more, we should not tackle other changes in routine that may be

upsetting. It is no time to start toilet training, nor to change the bedtime routine because you want the child to sleep alone. We can tackle those after we've got pretty good control of tantrums.

7. *Nagging, shaming, and verbal abuse have no place in the handling of tantrums*
Such behavior is not only ineffective, but often exacerbates the tantrum. For example, children often get more extreme in their tantrums in order to shut off the parents' nagging. Moreover, you would only be showing the child how you deal with people, teaching him new ways to tantrum, and encouraging him to do the same.

Thumbsucking

It is surprising how many parents are concerned about thumbsucking – about one in every eight parents report that their child has a thumbsucking "problem." The folklore on the topic truly borders on the absurd, as various authors have claimed it is associated with everything from masturbation to insecurity to dental problems. A closer look at the literature reveals that thumbsucking is . . . well . . . thumbsucking – nothing more, nothing less, and very rarely anything to worry about. It usually just goes away by itself, with no ill aftereffects.

Definition, incidence, norms, and reasons for thumbsucking
During the first three to four months of life, sucking is virtually the only way infants get food and drink, and it remains the principal method throughout the first year. Moreover, they appear to enjoy it even when it's not associated with food, as they will suck on your finger, pacifiers, and just about anything else (no matter how big or little, slimy or grotesque) that gets near their mouth. The mouth in fact will remain a magical source of pleasure for the rest of the child's life, as he graduates to licking, gum-chewing, nail-biting, and of course kissing.
Thumbsucking often starts during the early months, sometimes during the teething period, and occasionally later on in

imitation of a younger brother or sister. The child may often twist his hair, rub a cheek, pull on an ear, or hold a diaper or blanket in front of his face while sucking a thumb (or finger).

Thumbsucking generally peaks at 18-21 months of age, although there is a tremendous range as to its frequency and how long it lasts. Some children may suck for hours on end, either alone or watching other children play. Ordinarily, the habit will fade by two to three years of age, but it may persist until five or six years of age or beyond. Approximately 28 percent of children do continue beyond their third birthday, but it is relatively rare beyond five to six years of age.

Thumbsucking is often associated with sleep, as many children only suck their thumb when falling asleep or during sleep. However, some have also suggested that thumbsucking is at times associated with stress, insecurities in a child, or a lack if warmth or stimulation from parents – but all of these notions have proven to be false.

Alleged ill effects
Many kinds of problems have been attributed to thumbsucking. It has been said to lead to dental irregularities, infection, stomach disorders, and even masturbation. Infection and stomach disorders are prevented with the most basic of parenting skills – cleaning the child, preventing access to dangerous objects and substances, etc. The notion of masturbation is absurd and not worthy of further comment. A concern about dental irregularities, however, is common among parents and a real potential problem, though, as we will see, somewhat overrated.

Thumbsucking may displace the young teeth, though it would require fairly persistent pressure (thumbsucking). It can also cause callouses on the thumb, and the thumb may become infected. Aside from this, it has no known harmful effects. It does not cause problems in air swallowing, oral infections, or stomach problems – these are no more frequent in children who suck their thumbs than in children who do not.

Thumbsucking is much less often a source of dental problems than is generally thought. Heredity is by far the most important determinant of the quality, shape, and alignment of the teeth.

Moreover, since thumbsucking usually stops by the age of three, it usually does not influence the *permanent* teeth. Nonetheless, thumbsucking can in fact influence the teeth and palate (for example, sometimes causing "buck teeth"), especially if it is very persistent beyond the age of three. If you are concerned about the child's teeth, you should consult a dentist to find out if it is having a significant negative impact (as well as to get any recommendations the dentist may have about whether it is important to stop it, and how to stop it).

When is it a problem?
It becomes a problem – an unattractive and undesirable habit – in three situations. First, if it continues at five to six years of age (even then, however, if it only occurs at bedtime, I wouldn't worry about if for a while). Second, if a dentist reveals it is having a negative impact on the child's teeth. Third, after the age of two, if it becomes so excessive that it prevents play with peers, toys, or family, then it should be dealt with. Under the age of two, I simply wouldn't worry about it (or else, try different pacifiers).

How to handle thumbsucking
The most common way to handle thumbsucking is to interrrupt it, say "No thumbsucking," and distract the child with toys or activities. This, essentially, requires you to "shadow" a child – to sit or stand next to the child, ready to block the arm (with your arm or hand) *from going into* the mouth, and gently pulling the thumb out whenever the child beats you to the punch. Taking the hand out need not involve yelling, startling, or any special firmness – we simply want to interrupt it, and then prevent it from recurring. This takes some time, attention, and effort on your part, as you will play with the child to distract him, and shadow him (watching for the arm to move toward the mouth and blocking it or bringing it back down). But it does usually work.

An alternative is to put a bad-tasting substance on the thumb, and several are commercially available to the public. Some writers have claimed that this may be too unkind, or it may arouse negativism. In a two- to three-year-old, negativism is much more apt to occur from the previous interruption (shadowing) procedure, because in that case *you* are constantly stopping the child and he may get mad at you for it. With the present procedure, if you put the substance on while he is still asleep each morning (so he can't relate your painting his thumb to the bad taste), the young child simply finds that the thumb doesn't taste good any more, and it's no fun to suck. (If a restaurant changes chefs and you don't like the spaghetti sauce anymore, you don't eat there.) And there are no emotional or adjustment problems whatsoever; to the contrary, the child may socialize and talk *more*, now that his thumb is out of his mouth.

A third procedure, recommended by some dentists as well as psychologists, is to actually prevent thumbsucking for a period of time, in order to break the habit. This can be done by sewing up the sleeves of his pyjamas, or putting mittens on (and tying them on). This may or may not work, as the child may revert to thumbsucking when the mittens are removed. It might be helpful, if you decide to use this procedure, to introduce other enjoyable activities that give oral gratification when the mittens are on, in the hope that these activities will replace thumbsucking – perhaps a pacifier for a young child, gum-chewing for an older child, or some other activity you feel your child may enjoy.

A final strategy involves the use of rewards. If the thumbsucking is of sufficient concern, we can say "I'll give you a surprise if you don't suck your thumb." At first we might give that surprise after only 15 minutes if the child refrains from thumbsucking, and then gradually build it up to 30 minutes, one hour, 2 hours, etc. Of course, the child is also praised lavishly when he refrains from thumbsucking for the proper length of time. In difficult cases, one can add to this a cost – for example, "You can only suck your thumb in your room." But this should *only* be used if there are many enjoyable things to do in the living room or outside, so the child does *not* want to go to his room to suck his thumb (he'd be missing too much and it's not worth it).

It would be unkind to do these procedures at any time other than the three problem situations we have described. In these three situations, none of the procedures is unkind – they are *helping* the child. I'm not sure which is more intrusive or upsetting – preventing it, interrupting it, or putting a bitter tasting substance on the thumb – and a parent should use whichever he or she feels most comfortable with. The bad-tasting substance is more convenient – you don't have to watch or shadow the child during the procedure – if convenience is an issue to you. In any case, nagging, shaming, and yelling are neither required nor effective. They have no place in the treatment of thumbsucking (or any other behavior in this book).

A final note. Some dentists I spoke with won't touch thumbsucking until eight to nine years of age. At that age, some recommend the use of a "wire cage fixed to the upper molars behind the front teeth, to stop the thumb from touching the palate". In my opinion, thumbsucking that is persistent and/or interferes with play and social activities is already a problem, and should not be left for eight to nine years. The child may be ostracized by his peers, fail to learn social and play skills, and may feel left out or even "inferior." I view a wire cage as a last resort, if the other procedures do not work. And I would definitely intervene much earlier than the age of eight or nine, if thumbsucking is a persistent habit that interferes with play and social activities, or it is causing dental problems.

Speech

Children's speech takes time to develop, and they will make lots of mistakes along the way. All children will *stutter* – repeating words, stammering, hesitating in certain situations, or "blocking" on certain words. All children will have a difficult time *articulating* some words properly, and they will talk too fast at times, "*cluttering*" their speech (tripping over their words and getting them jumbled up). And (the biggie) some children will *learn to talk later* than others. While all of these can become problems, they rarely do. For most children, it is a step along the way to normal language – as they continue to mature, physically and intellectually, they improve, expand, and refine their speech.

Fully 95 percent of our children have no real problem whatsoever in speech. They do stutter, clutter, mispronounce, leave off a few syllables, and generally murder the language along the way, but these are just developmental phases children go through – they soon disappear. At the same time, this does not mean that we can't improve a child's speech. We can always encourage politeness ("say please"), teach new words, and encourage new verbal skills for problem solving and for new social situations.

Let's look at these speech difficulties individually to distinguish when each is and is not a problem, and what we can do to help.

Stuttering

i. Definition and incidence
Stuttering is characterized by interruptions in the flow of speech. A child may "block" on a word and be unable to say it, he may hesitate before each word, be unable to articulate certain sounds, or else repeat sounds and words excessively. Stuttering may increase when a child is excited, tired, afraid or under stress, or else she just may not have mastered a certain word or sound yet.

Stuttering occurs most frequently in the two to four age group, after which it declines. One study of 200 two- to four-year-old normal preschoolers showed that every single one of them stuttered, and in fact about one of every four words was a repetition of some sort – "M-m-mommy, may I have a coo-cookie?"

Despite being such a prevalent behavior in early childhood, the fact is that only about one percent of children continue to stutter with any regularity beyond the age of ten.

ii. When is stuttering a problem?
Normal children between two and four years of age love to use their new and growing speech skills. At 36 months, they *average 15,000 words per day* – it's like a dam burst. Since this is the same age group that will repeat on the average one out of every four words, there may be an incredible frequency of repetition – several thousand perhaps. It's not surprising then that at this age many parents become concerned about a possible stuttering problem. Rest assured it is quite normal, a phase that most children pass right through and never look back on.

To put it in perspective, stuttering would not usually be considered a problem unless the child was at least five years of age, with at least ten (and often as many as 1000) dysfluences per day, *each* day, for an extended period of time (i.e. six months). Moreover, a stuttering problem is often specific to certain situations, sounds, places, or people. For example, if a child is afraid of school (or animals, the dark, etc.), he may stutter only while talking about school or while he is at school. Similarly, if a child stutters only when she is stressed or upset, she may be fluent most of the time but begin to stammer when extra demands are placed on her, or when she has to do something that she dislikes (go to the dentist, go to bed, go to school). On the other hand, sometimes the stuttering is specific to certain sounds or words, or to long words in general. In such cases, after five years of age, the stuttering is a problem that needs to be dealt with.

iii. How to handle stuttering

We shouldn't make a big deal of stuttering in young children, or else they will probably become self-conscious, more hesitant in their speech rather than less so, and a real problem of stuttering may well develop *because* of our efforts. The best way to handle it is not to handle it at all, at least in the very large majority of children under five years of age.

It is sad to say that the public-at-large doesn't know a great deal about stuttering, and people who stutter are often assumed to be abnormal or inferior in other ways . . . even mentally deficient. Let me put your mind to rest: *this is utter nonsense.* There is no relationship whatsoever between stuttering and intelligence (IQ); stuttering does not imply, suggest, or in any way mean that a child (or adult) is abnormal or inferior. I emphasize this not just to make you feel better, but in the hope that you will not caution your child about it, or otherwise draw his attention to it. This could make the child self-conscious, perpetuate and heighten the stuttering, and *make* her feel inferior. Let me give an example to illustrate how this can happen.

One case I read about concerns Jimmy, who was regarded as a superior speaker. He was a leader among his peers, quite bright, and he had in fact won a number of speaking contests. He then changed to another school where a "speech examiner" tested him. The first time they met, she made a tape of his speech; the second time, she played the tape for Jimmy and told him he was a stutterer.

Most children will stammer if you tell them they're going to be taped, if they think it is important or an evaluation of some kind. Jimmy was nervous, as most children would be. The untrained teacher misjudged Jimmy who was, after all, a superior speaker.

Unfortunately, Jimmy took the diagnosis to heart. The teacher told him to speak slowly, to watch himself, to try to control his speech, to relax . . . Jimmy's parents were beside themselves, terribly upset. Speech was one of his special talents; what had happened? So they set out dedicated to help Jimmy, reminding him of every little slip or hesitation.

If you give a person this much instruction on how to walk, he'd soon be tripping over his own feet. And this is what happened to Jimmy. He developed a quite serious case of stuttering – he became tense, jerky, hesitant, apprehensive, "tripping" over every other word.

Under the age of five, we should usually just leave a child's stuttering alone; 99 percent of children will simply outgrow it. This is not to say, however, that we can't speak to a speech therapist or child psychologist about it. If you are concerned (about stuttering or any other behavior), you shouldn't hesitate to seek information, opinions, and advice from a professional. In most cases, a professional will be able to reassure you; for the one percent of children who do need help, that help can be planned at a very early stage, maximizing the chances of a successful treatment.

If, at the age of five or later, a real problem of stuttering is suspected – consistently high rates of dysfluency over a period of six months, often associated with certain fearful situations, upsetting events, or else focused on certain kinds of sounds or words – then one should consult with a child psychologist or speech therapist to get additional information or assistance.

If a child is five or older, and stuttering is in fact a pervasive problem, then it should be treated. There are many possible side-effects of stuttering, as a child feels more and more uncomfortable in school, doesn't participate, and falls behind his peers; he may avoid speaking as much as possible; he may avoid social situations, out of embarassment, and therefore normal friendships and social skills don't develop; he may be teased a lot, develop a poor self-image, think he is inferior to others his age. Such side-effects can be prevented, if we deal with the problem quickly and effectively.

A tremendous body of research has shown that stuttering can be treated; success rates are very high. Furthermore, there are no known aftereffects – if it is caught early and treated properly, the stuttering usually disappears with no repercussions on social functioning, school, friendships, or damage to the child's confidence and self-esteem.

Treatment procedures that have been shown to be successful are described in Table 4-2. While these are the most common approaches to treatment, they should not be tried on your own. An experienced speech therapist or child psychologist is needed to get the proper treatment in place. With professional assistance, however, studies have shown high rates of treatment success, with the Habit Control procedure curing each (100 percent) of 14 stutterers who ranged in age from four to 65, and who ranged from two to a thousand episodes of stuttering per day.

In short, most children under the age of five will simply grow out of it if we leave them alone. For those children who do continue to stutter, or who suffer anxiety because of it, treatment procedures are available.

Delayed Speech

Many parents become anxious about when their child should begin to talk. Some even try to push their child, wanting him to talk early – which would mean of course that he is a "bright" child. And God forbid if the child's speech comes a bit later than in other children – that would mean he must be "slow." Neither of these are true, of course, unless language comes *extremely* early or late. For example, Table 4-3 illustrates a number of common milestones in speech development. These are averages, so this means that about half of all children *will* show these

---

Table 4-2

The most common treatment procedures for stuttering:

---

1. *Delayed Auditory Feedback (DAF)*. When one's own speech is fed back through headphones, it can delay hearing what we said for a fraction of a second. This slows down our speech, and prolongs each word. For many stutterers it eliminates the dysfluencies, producing slow, prolonged, fluent speech.

2. *Metronome*. Speaking in time to a beat, such as a metronome, has been known to produce a marked (though often temporary) improvement in fluency.

3. *Shadowing*. Stuttering is greatly reduced when the person is asked to repeat or read a passage right *after* another person has just read it. In this way he practices normal fluent speech.

4. *Habit Control Package*. This is a relatively new and very exciting treatment for stuttering. It contains a number of components: teaching the child which specific situations produce stuttering, so the child can come to recognize and anticipate it ahead of time; relaxation training to handle any tension associated with stuttering; teaching activities that are incompatible with stuttering – stop speaking for a minute and take slow deep breaths, formulate mentally the words before speaking them, emphasize the first few words in a sentence, speak for short durations – and practising these procedures and fluent speech in a variety of situations.

---

milestones later than those shown in the table, and half will show them earlier. That a child should begin to talk later than average does *not* mean he is "duller" or less intelligent. It will be comforting, then, to know what is a normal delay and what is a "severe" delay.

Table 4-3
Milestones in speech development:

3-6 months	babbling, mostly vowel sounds
6-9 months	has up to 12 sounds; uses mostly vowels; may imitate 1 or 2 sounds
14-15 months	has up to 3 words; uses 18 sounds or more; vocalizes frequently; imitates easily
24 months	has 250-300 words; uses 25 different sounds; averages about 75 words per hour during free play; uses 2- or 3- word phrases (I want a cookie, up daddy, ball game); names common objects; uses some pronouns (I, me mine,it, that, who)
36 months	uses up to 900 words in simple 3-4-word sentences; averages 15,000 words per day; can repeat 2 or 3 numbers from memory; asks questions; begins to tell stories; begins to use plurals
48 months	uses up to 1,500 words in sentences averaging 5 words in length; averages 400 words per hour; counts to 3; names colors; relates fanciful tales; questioning is at a peak ("Why," "How"); sings songs; repeats 4 numbers from memory

---

i. Definition and incidence of speech delay
Exactly when a child meets each milestone is less important than seeing a generally improving trend in speech development. That is, during the first 15 months you should see an increase in the amount of vocalizing, and in the number of different sounds a child makes; from 15 months to 48 months you should see a steady expansion in the number of words, and the length of phrases, a child uses. Whether the child has six sounds or 12 sounds at six months, whether she has 25 words or 250 words at two years of age, is simply not that important. What is important

is whether the child's speech is steadily improving: he's making more and more sounds, more and more words, using longer and longer phrases, etc. As long as a child is progressing steadily, you need not worry; it is only when progress slows or stops for any length of time that we will be concerned about a possible speech delay.

Viewed in this way, it is indeed very rare for children to have a "speech delay." Studies show that about 99.8 percent of children do not have a speech delay; only two out of 1,000 children do. This shows that while half of all children will meet language milestones a bit later than those shown in Table 4-3, it simply doesn't mean anything. The vast majority progress rapidly, even if it's a few months later; they learn to talk, and are normal in every respect.

ii. When a delay in speech development is a problem
In general, there are two major signs of a speech-delayed child. First, the most common milestone used to indicate a speech delay focuses on when a child begins to use words. In general, if a child does not have at least five words by the age of 24 months, a speech program should be started. Second, if at any time the child falls a year behind, one should seek professional consultation. Let's take these one at a time.

Many children begin to use their first words at about 14-15 months, some as much as four to six months earlier. At two years of age, however, children should be regularly using words, although there is a tremendous amount of variability in the number of words they use. In one study with normal two-year-olds, the authors found that one child used as few as five words while another used as many as 1200 words – the average was 250-300 words. Clearly, there is tremendous variability in the rate of speech development of normal children. Yet, it would be quite unusual for a child to have fewer than five words at this time, and professional consultation should be obtained to at least monitor the situation, or plan a treatment if necessary.

In general, other kinds of speech delay are quite rare; most often, if a child begins to use words in a meaningful way, she is "over the hump" and will continue to progress normally. On occasion, however, one may find slow rates of progress (for example, if there is a hearing loss, retardation, head injuries), or possibly even regression or loss of previous language skills (for example, in autism). If a child falls 12 months behind in achieving the milestones for speech development, medical or psychological consultation should be obtained.

In most cases, there will be other signs that there is a problem, and a parent will know there is "something wrong." The child with retardation will be slow in other areas, not just with speech; the child with a head injury may lose motor co-ordination, appear confused or forgetful, and not understand things said to him; the autistic child will lack affection, and engage in persistent, repetitive motor movements (i.e. finger-flapping, intense body rocking); and so on. If your child is developing normally in most areas – understanding what you say, motor skills, social skills – then normal speech will probably come a bit later. (One may still of course seek some advice from a professional, for reassurance and to keep an eye on the situation).

iii. What can we do to promote speech?

It is interesting to note that the "only child" (no brothers or sisters), who has a lot of adult contact, becomes the most proficient at speech. Why? It is "modelling" and "opportunity" that are without a doubt the most important things we can provide. The best way to encourage a child's speech is to talk to the child . . . a lot . . . and give him a chance to talk. Sounds simple, doesn't it? And yet, much of the time children talk, parents don't listen (they're doing something else, talking to someone else); they interrupt a child before he's finished; or they give short answers because they've got something to do or somewhere to go. In addition, parents often do things for a child before he asks, perhaps because we already know what he's thinking – we know he wants something ("Are you hungry?"), or we know he's frustrated or in need ("I'll help you."). The result is, he doesn't have to talk to get what he wants: his talking is being ignored, and there are few opportunities to talk (to practise words, and new creative combinations of them).

If we instead are more careful to initiate "conversations" each day, listen and let the child finish, ask questions, react to what the child says, then we will be providing lots of attention for talking, lots of models for new words, and lots of opportunity for the child to use speech, practise it, create and experiment with it, and discover how it can be used to get information, solve problems, invent stories, play games, etc.

One additional factor will be of tremendous help. We must praise the child for any and all vocalizations, to let her know that speech is (greatly) appreciated. As the child vocalizes more and more, we can praise the better, longer, and more advanced utterances – words, then word combinations, phrases, etc. In this way, we're not only presenting a warm stimulating environment for speech, but we're specifically shaping more and better speech production.

A final note. If a child has no words at two years of age, it is a serious problem. Unfortunately, many pediatricians, child psychologists, and assessment clinics do not recognize the seriousness of it, and are leery to prescribe treatment at such a young age. I can't tell you how many parents have been told "the child will probably grow out of it," only to be faced with the grim diagnosis of social or intellectual retardation a short year later. The truth is this – if speech therapy begins at two, the child might be brought up to normal language levels; a further delay of a year (he's already a year behind) becomes very difficult to overcome. *Do not take no for an answer* – get help (speech therapy) for that child at two years of age. More often than not, the child will *not* simply grow out of it, and treatment is a must.

Articulation
Maturation serves as a natural cure for most articulation difficulties; pronunciation errors in young children rarely persist. All children leave off the final consonants of some words ("buy" for bike), skip syllables altogether ("nana" for banana), substitute one sound for another ("kickle" for tickle), or otherwise murder words ("sgettee" for spaghetti). Articulation will continue to improve until the age of nine or ten with no special intervention; problems that exist beyond that are likely to persist unless treatment is given.

i. Definition, incidence, and causes

All the textbooks will tell you that articulation difficulties represent the largest category of all speech problems. They certainly do represent the most common *concern* about speech, and it represents up to 75 percent of all children referred to a speech therapist. Yet, rarely is it a real problem in young children. Articulation improves naturally with age, up until about the fourth grade. *Only two percent of children continue to have articulation problems beyond the fourth grade.*

An articulation problem refers to faulty sound production or faulty use of sounds. It will occur in all children, in one or more of its several forms – substituting one sound for another, running sounds together so they are incomprehensible, omitting certain syllables in a word, etc. Children simply aren't born as masters of the language – it develops gradually, and errors are fundamental to the learning process.

Most articulation errors are part of the learning process, part of language development – rarely are they due to organic flaws (malformed mouth, jaw, or teeth; nerve injury; etc.). On occasion, they can persist a bit because the environment encourages it – we should not get too carried away with how "cute" and funny those mispronunciations can be; it may be time to ease off on our "baby talk," as the child can be picking it up from us. But in general, it is usually nothing to worry about. There is typically a sharp decrease in the frequency of articulation errors during the first three years of school, and such speech inaccuracies have no known effect on achievement, social relationships, or anything else, in children under the age of six.

Fears and phobias

Most children do have fears, lots of fears, so you should not be taken aback by them. In fact, almost half (43 percent) of all parents are concerned because their child has *multiple* fears. Most of these fears will disappear, and then they will be replaced by new ones. As the child gets older, his imagination, thinking, creativity, and understanding are growing so rapidly that there are new things to fear. As the child gets older, she discovers that dogs can bite (and it hurts); that in the darkness he can be startled, bump into things, or trip and fall; that she can't breathe underwater; that there may be strange-looking creatures with three eyes, super strength, or a taste for blood that live on other planets and visit him in his sleep. And they all seem so real, so close, to the young child. As he grows older, however, he realizes that darkness does not bring out the monsters; and he gains more mastery in the water and with animals. He masters what he is afraid of, or else learns that there really is nothing to fear. *As long as the child keeps replacing his fears – no one fear lasts too long – there is little to be concerned about.*

While fears are common in children, phobias are not. A phobia is much more than a fear. Normal childhood fears lessen and disappear with time; if instead they continue to get stronger, scarier, and more intense over time, there could be a phobia.

While phobias are rare in children, when they do occur, they can have disturbing side-effects. The child who is afraid of water, for example, may refuse to go near a swimming pool, participate with other children in water-play, and come to feel inferior or become the butt of some cruel jokes or funny looks from other children.

At the same time, phobias are relatively easy to treat, especially in young children. To give an example, my son developed a phobia for hospitals and doctors, a very severe phobia, probably much more serious than most young children (and their parents) will have to face. And it was "treated" quite easily and successfully by the naturally occurring exposure, and even pleasant experiences, that later occurred in hospitals and with doctors.

When my son was three years old, he broke his leg. It was a severe break, and the hospital experience was quite traumatic. At the hospital, they had to straighten his broken leg (make sure the bones were aligned), bandage it, put a splint on it, and then (later) put a cast on it. They moved the leg about to take an x-ray, change the sheets, clean him, and replace the bandages and splint, etc. – all of which was very painful, at least for the first few weeks. I'll never forget when they first had to straighten his leg. After a nurse first saw him in the emergency room, and rushed him ahead of all those people who had been waiting for hours (I knew we were in for trouble), the doctor asked us to hold his arms down, tightly. As the doctor pulled here and pushed there on the leg – with my son shrieking in pain, screaming "No! No!" – I know it didn't help him seeing the tears, anguish, trembling, and utter helplessness on the faces of mommy and daddy. No wonder he became absolutely phobic about hospitals, doctors, nurses, examination rooms, x-rays, and even those white coats they wear. We thought he would never get over it; we were just sure that such an intensely upsetting experience would leave enduring scars and fears.

It didn't. So many "natural" positive experiences with hospitals and doctors followed that the fears faded and disappeared – to our utter amazement. About four months after getting out of the hospital, he (reluctantly) went to the hospital to see mommy and his brand-new baby sister, and he had a ball there watching, touching, holding, and talking to his new baby sister – although he was *very* upset at leaving mommy in "that hospital" when he went home for the night.

Shortly thereafter, he developed a severe case of asthma and was having trouble breathing. Off we went to the (gulp) same hospital, with much trepidation, where lo and behold they gave him a "ventolin mask" which quickly cleared his breathing and made him feel "great." Later, when we went to see the doctor for regular physical examinations, we took time to play with all the gizmos and gadgets – looking in each other's ears, listening to our heartbeats, using the blood-pressure cuff, building stick-figures with tongue depressors – and he learned that going to the doctor didn't always hurt. With no special "treatment" whatsoever, this very severe phobia virtually disappeared within two years.

The point is that this fear was much more intense than most young children will ever experience, and yet it still just faded away naturally over time. The same is true of most childhood fears.

Definition of fears and phobias
In general, a child is said to be afraid of something if she *consistently* reacts emotionally to it, and tries to avoid it. All children

are afraid of some things, and it can show up in different ways. Young infants show a startle reponse, blink their eyes, arch their backs, and may begin to cry when they hear a loud noise, see a flash of light, or lose support to the back or head. Older children may cry, become shy or timid, hide behind a parent's legs, or run away when they see a dog, thunder and lightning, or a stranger moving toward them.

Such fears are quite normal, and nothing to worry about – they are simply developmental phases that children pass through until they gain some mastery and understanding of animals, water, darkness, and fantasy. These fears should, however, change over time. Each fear should be easing, diminishing, even if another fear crops up while this is happening. What is important is that a given fear should ease in intensity over time, rather than building up, getting stronger, or more intense. For example, "eight-month stranger anxiety" is quite common in a child six to nine months old. And yet, if a three-year-old is still afraid of strangers, refuses to speak in their presence, or flees the scene, even when her parents are there, then it would be considered a problem. In short, if a fear is strengthening over time, instead of weakening, it is a problem that should be dealt with.

In order to be called a phobia, a fear must also be *irrational*. If there is any real danger, of course, the fear should not be considered a phobia. No one should set out to eradicate all fear – fear can be a useful safety measure, to remove us from danger. It is only a phobia when there is extreme fear in a situation in which there is actually little or no danger. If a child walks two blocks out of his way to avoid a dog that is on a leash, in a yard, or behind a fence, it is not rational. On the other hand, if he sees a gaunt, unkempt, skinny dog running toward him growling, salivating, and showing his teeth, with his eyes going in different directions, then a goodly amount of fear would be quite appropriate.

In addition to being irrational, the fear must interfere with common everyday activities. We all have fears, but in the large majority of people it is not a problem. Our fear of snakes, airplanes, heights, and spiders may be relatively mild, not interfering with normal activities. Perhaps the child is anxious for a while about school, but goes anyway. Perhaps he is afraid of snakes, but rarely sees one.

Sometimes, however, a fear can be both irrational and debilitating: the child who is so afraid of school that he refuses to go, runs away, feigns illness, stands alone off by himself when he is there, or refuses to talk, play, or sit with other children (and this is not the first day of school, or a new school); the child who is afraid of dirt or germs and spends much of his free time washing, instead of playing; the child who is so preoccupied with sickness or death that she remains sad and doesn't want to play or eat. If such fears get worse and worse, rather than easing over time, then they would be considered phobias. This is relatively rare in young children, but if it should occur we must help the child, and the earlier the better (see "Early intervention," pages 11-14).

Incidence of common fears

Virtually all kids have fears; in fact, in one study almost one-half of the parents reported that their children had seven or more fears. It seems to begin in early infancy, and continue right through the age of 12.

In early infancy (up to six months), babies are primarily afraid of any startling noise or movement; loss of support; sudden or intense stimulation; and new, novel, or unexpected things or events. Then, at around eight months, babies are commonly very afraid of unfamiliar people – it is so common for infants to be apprehensive and upset with strange adults during this time, it has been called "eight-month stranger anxiety." This should, however, subside within several months. After that, between nine and 24 months, the most common fears are about separation from parents, injury, and the toilet. This is a time when children are bothered by being wet, and by soiled diapers; they're beginning to walk, and there are many falls, bumps, and bruises along the way; and parents are beginning to put the child to bed while they are still awake, rather than holding them or rocking them to sleep.

Between 24 and 48 months, a child's fears come more from

imagination rather than physical causes. And the imagination can run wild! The most common fears are about darkness, imaginary creatures, dogs, being alone – and don't be surprised to see him take a three-eyed, scaly, gigantic, slimy, serpent-like, man-eating, ghost-like monster quite seriously.

During the fifth and sixth years, fears about school, sickness, fires, thunder and lightning, insects, and dirt are the most common. At this age, having by now mastered many of the imaginary creatures, a child is more concerned about real things, from dirt to bugs to school.

These are just the most common fears, and the most common times at which they occur. There are an infinite number of possible fears, and these may occur at different times in different children. So, if your child is afraid of fire engines, elevators, or water, there is no cause for alarm. The major issues are how intense or incapacitating the fears are, and how long they last, not what the child is afraid of.

Such fears usually subside over time, although the length of time needed may vary – stranger anxiety in the eight-month old should subside within months, while a fear of dogs (perhaps the most common of all fears) may not subside until the child is seven or eight years old. Most of the fears will require between a few weeks (a fear of preschool) up to six to 12 months to subside. Some fears, however, are a bit more tenacious and persistent, such as fears involving physical illness, or fears of social situations (i.e. meeting people, group play). These we should keep a leisurely eye on, as they may not subside at all.

Most important, children have a *much* better chance of overcoming fears, even phobias, than do adults. So it is helpful to deal with them early if they (a fear or a phobia) are a concern. The treatment is neither upsetting to the child, nor difficult to do. Relatively brief intervention has been highly successful in more than 80 percent of phobic children. The prognosis is, in short, extremely good, even for an extremely fearful (phobic) child.

Why do these fears develop?
Well-known experiments by Ivan Pavlov illustrate the most common ways fears develop, through "pairing." If every time an

animal hears a bell, it is followed by (paired with) an electric shock, the animal will become terrified of bells. In a similar fashion, if parents leave the child alone consistently when it is dark – that is, when we put a child to bed – a child may come to be afraid of the dark, since it's always associated with mommy leaving. This may be why darkness is such a natural, common fear. If bad things happen at preschool, one can develop a fear of school. If one is scared of or startled by a dog, taken to a hospital whenever he's hurt (as we all are), or upset and missing grandpa when he passed away, the child may become fearful of dogs, hospitals and sickness, or death. And it may take very few pairings for a fear to develop, especially if it is a traumatic episode.

There are other ways fears and phobias develop, and some are very subtle. Just as we learn about values, ethics, and morals from parents and friends, so too can children learn their fears. We see, hear, or read about the bad things that happen in a swimming pool (drownings), while playing sports (injuries) – and no one talks about the other eight million children who go swimming and play sports; nothing happens to them except they have fun. Our children pick up our concerns from the way we react, the warnings we give them, and from what they see us and others do. If a child sees mommy dip her toe in the water and shake with fear – followed by "No Way!" and an abrupt departure – the child is not going to go gleefully skipping into the water. If daddy sees a snake, scrunches up his face, takes a step back, and tries (unsuccessfully) to suppress a "yech," the child is not going to bend over and pet this new "thing." If mom and dad talk at dinner about that child in the newspaper who got stuck for six hours in an elevator, how sad it was, what a nice kid he was, and that he was in many ways like "our son," your child will probably have a conniption the next time you ask him to go in an elevator. Moreover, your child will see other children being afraid of different things – at preschool, at daycare, at home, and at play – and children will often imitate each other's fears.

There are many ways that fears develop, and it would be virtually impossible to try preventing them – you can't sleep with your child forever, and you can't avoid preschools, daycares, playmates, or television, for the most part. The two areas where parents can help to prevent fears are, first, trying not to discuss scary episodes in front their child; and, second, trying not to show when they're squeamish and what they're squeamish about . . . if they can.

Handling fears

To handle children's fears, we must separate two kinds of situations. First, there is the fear that is momentary, transient, like a child waking up at night from nightmares. This is not a problem – it will pass – but we still need to help the child through it. The second situation represents the fear that is a potential concern, the anxiety that persists and grows and that might have a detrimental effect on our child over the long run if we let it go on too long.

In the first case – transient fears – our reaction will be to comfort and calm our anxious child. If the fear has to do with nightmares, storms, or imaginary monsters, that's all we'll have to do: as the child grows, these fears will pass. The only question here is how to comfort them, not whether to comfort them. There is no excuse whatsoever for parents who say, "He'll learn if we just leave him alone"; "He'll live"; "There are no hobgoblins, monsters, or ghosts, and there's *nothing* to be afraid of, so this is the last time I'm coming in here"; etc. The child is *really* afraid, illogical though it may be to you, and it does no good to let the child remain afraid . . . and alone. Since the fear is irrational, he can *not* be talked out of it, no matter how obvious it is to you that there is no danger. It is very real to the child, and any further suffering is unnecessary (and preventable). Moreover, many of us want to teach our children that we'll be there in time of need – and ignoring his fears will teach him something quite different.

So we jump when a child is afraid of storms, has nightmares, or sees ghosts. We can sit with her, hold her, talk to her, read a story, rock her to sleep, even lay down with her. We can show him there are no ghosts under the bed, and explain how his/her heroes (Barbie, He-Man, Big Bird) and friends (stuffed animals or puppets) laugh at ghosts, and destroy them just by staring at them. We can bring in a night-light to brighten up the room; and put his superheroes, dolls, and teddy bears on the dresser, on his bed against the wall, and in the doorway to protect him from any monsters. We can tell her that we used to be afraid of ghosts, too, but that we found out that they sleep at night. We can put a magic crystal, swords, laser guns next to his bed. We can check to see if she heard any scary stories at school, read a story, or saw a TV show that could have frightened her – and make sure they do not recur for the next few days. We do not do *all* of these things, of course – or it might make it look like there's really something to be afraid of – we just *try* these things until we find some that comfort and calm him, while keeping a playful, confident, and relaxed manner about us. Most of all, we just do what's necessary to comfort the child, perhaps staying with him, rocking him, or holding hands, until he falls back to sleep.

Now let's turn to the kinds of fears that may be of more concern to parents – when a child's anxiety seems to be getting more severe as time passes, rather than diminishing – such as a growing fear of school, water, being alone, dogs, or social situations. The most effective way to eliminate the fear is with a procedure called "Participant Modelling." The principle here is to break down the fear into small steps and tackle them one at a time. We start with the least upsetting situation and gradually work up to the more stressful ones. In addition, we comfort, talk to, hold hands, demonstrate for the child at each step, giving lots of encouragement and praise for each new advance no matter how small. This can be done with almost anything the child is afraid of, but let's use two examples, a fear of a swimming pool and a fear of school, to illustrate the procedure.

If the child is the slightest bit nervous ten feet from the swimming pool, we stop there. We talk, play with toys, relax, until he is completely at ease. Then we take a step closer and, if he again gets a bit anxious, we stop again and play. At each step, it can take two minutes or 20 minutes for the child to relax, but we do not proceed until he is relaxed. He will relax; the fear will dissipate and extinguish. When he does take each new step, we praise him lavishly. We continue doing this, step by step, until we get to the edge of the pool. Then, we sit down on the edge, and put our feet on the top step. If the child resists, we don't force him – we encourage him by putting our own feet in, splashing the water and laughing, putting toys in the pool, etc., until he does. If you just wait, patiently, giving encouragement periodically, he will do it as he relaxes and feels more at ease, and the longer he just sits at the edge, the more comfortable he will become. Then, we stand up, go to the second step, then the third, in the same fashion. When he is standing in the shallow end, holding on to the side of the pool, we can lift him in our arms and go for a walk in the pool, splashing, playing, pointing out what other children are doing and what fun they're having. As he relaxes and becomes more playful and venturesome, we can put our face against the water for an instant, blow bubbles, etc. in a playful manner, encouraging him to do the same. This can continue, in small steps, in order to teach the child to swim if so desired.

Precisely the same principles can be used when a child is afraid of dogs (choose a dog that is as docile as possible), heights, fire engines, strangers, or school. In each case, we first find a situation that has very little fear (a parked fire truck, caged animals at the zoo, etc.), and then demonstrate for the child, praise him, progress through the steps at his own pace, encouraging him at every step. It may take a number of trips to the pool, or the school, but this method is successful with the very large majority of children.

Let's use a fear of going to school as our second example. First, we identify the situations in or about school that are most fearful. The first day (with the teacher's permission), we might go with him, play an enjoyable new game together for a half hour, and then take the child home. Hmm . . . that wasn't so bad. The next day, we again play together, but we play for an hour this time and then go home. The key of course is that your child should love it – because you're there and it's a new and enjoyable game. The third day, we might tell him that we need another child to play this game – who does he want? Invite that child over, and we all play together for 15 minutes of the hour. Then a different child comes during the next 15 minutes (one is replaced by another, so the child is getting to know each classmate). As this continues – the child is having fun at school –

we then pull in two children at a time to play, making sure that we are all having fun together. Then we ask the teacher (who of course has been consulted throughout) to join us off and on, for a few minutes each time, making sure that the teacher is sensitive to your child's anxiety and that she treats him very well. Then, we can say: "Oh, I have to go next door for a minute, but I'll be right back," thereby leaving your child with two other children and the teacher. (Tell the teacher you're going to do this, and do it at a time when the child is having fun and will not miss you, if possible.) Then we go away for gradually longer and longer periods ("I'll be back after this game"; "I'll be back at 11:00"; etc.).

The key is that each step must be a minor change from the last, so that no one step causes much anxiety at all. It is the overall sequencing of those steps that will take us from point A to point B – from a child who refuses to go to school, all the way to just dropping him off at school in the morning and picking him up when class is over . . . without a squeak. In fact, he will now be looking forward to seeing his friends.

Head-banging and other self-injurious behavior

Few things have ever scared me as much as seeing my child intentionally bang his head against the wall. Oh, I knew that many normal children engage in some form of self-injurious behavior . . . but it's a whole different ball game to see it in your own child, and it was hard to believe that this could possibly be normal. It is normal. In fact, it's so common that self-injurious behavior, in some form, occurs in most children during the first two years. It is very rarely severe or dangerous, however, just scary looking – and in the vast majority of children it simply goes away by itself.

Definition
Self-injurious behavior does not mean that a child necessarily hurts or injures himself. In fact, it is very rare for any injury to occur. It is called self-injury because it has the *potential* to do harm if it is done too intensely. For the most part, however, it is

rhythmical, repetitious, and mild, causing no harm whatsoever.

The most worrisome form of this behavior to most parents is head-banging – against the headboard or railing of the crib, the walls, floors, sofa, against the back of a highchair or forward (down) on its tray. Other forms include biting the lip, teeth-grinding, chewing the inside of the mouth (causing sores), hair-rubbing or pulling, biting the arm or hand, and scratching. In young children, up to 18 months of age, these are usually done repetitively, rhythmically, and with little intensity. In somewhat older children (two to six years of age), however, self-injurious behavior may be more troublesome – it may become more intense, less rhythmical and repetitive, and it may occur more for the attention and reaction it gets.

Incidence

This behavior often begins to appear at four to 12 months of age, and can remain a common occurrence up until the age of two years. It can last a few days, a week, a month, or for one or two years – there is no standard rule or norm. Teeth-grinding appears in a whopping 56 percent of youngsters, but is rarely a problem requiring treatment in this age group. Head-banging, biting, scratching, hair-pulling, self-hitting, *each* occur in 3 to 15 percent of children under the age of two years, and they occur three or four times more often in boys than in girls.

In short, there is a mighty good chance that a normal child will show one or another of these forms of self-injurious behavior. At the same time, it is *very* rare indeed for this behavior to cause any injury whatsoever in children under two years of age, and it typically decreases even if nothing is done and the behavior is left to run its own course.

Why does it occur?

These behaviors may start out in the young child as a form of "self-stimulation." That is, the child wants to stimulate himself – to do something, to feel something, to explore – and head-banging (believe it or not) provides a great deal of sensory stimulation. For example, there is the movement itself (which is often rhythmical, an added source of pleasure); then there is the stimulation to the head; and finally, there is the auditory stimulation both from vibration in the ear as well as from the sound of the contact.

While this may sound like pretty poor stuff (reasons) to you and me, we must remember that we are talking about a child with a very limited repertoire – he can't explore the environment or obtain stimulation by leaving the crib, talking, visiting friends, or going to the movies, and there are times when he is relatively confined (i.e. in the crib) and alone (i.e. at night). After they're tired of sucking their hands, kicking their legs, and watching the mobile, they try something else – and they may try head-banging, scratching themselves or biting.

It is notable that these children rarely bang their heads when they're being held, played with, or otherwise stimulated. It's not that head-banging is so great, it just seems like it's something that babies do for stimulation when there's not much else to do, and other available activities are finished with. In fact, such behavior most often occurs at nap or bedtime, when babies are of course less stimulated (because we want to let them sleep). The bottom line, however, is that this behavior is not usually intense enough to do any harm.

A second reason for such behavior is to get attention. It may occur *at first* by accident, or as part of a tantrum – the child who is upset, swings his arms, and accidentally hits himself; the child who is hungry and hits his head or hand on the tray or the back of the highchair. But what happens afterward? Mommy (or daddy) gets that food on the tray . . . fast! And we comfort, talk to, and soothe the child, until the food gets there. The child quickly learns that nice things happen when he bangs his head – people jump, someone comes over (pronto), someone talks to, plays with, or picks up and holds him. As a result, the child may do it again when the food isn't ready fast enough, or if he wants to be held.

When is it a problem ?

There are at least three situations which call for intervention, but all three are quite rare. It should be dealt with: (1) if the behavior continues beyond the second year; (2) the minute a child "uses" such behavior to get attention or to get his own way (i.e. he wants to eat, he wants a toy, etc.); (3) at any time or at any age where there is any real danger to the child.

I would not, however, be concerned with the mild, rhythmic, or accidental forms that typically occur in the first two years – these occur in many children, have no known ill-effects, and seem only to be something to do when there aren't many alternatives.

What can be done?
We'll react very differently to those episodes which are simply self-stimulation as opposed to those that are manipulative or used to get the child's way.

In the case of *self-injurious behavior which is mild, repetitious, and/or rhythmical* (self-stimulation), typically starting at four to 18 months, there are two simple precautions one can take. First, we can protect the child by padding railings and headboards – for example, buying "bumper pads." This will ensure that the child *couldn't* hurt himself. (Similarly, one could cut the child's nails short in the case of scratching, put on a hat for a while in the case of hair-rubbing or pulling, etc.). Second, we can rock a child to sleep, hold his hand, sit or lay with him, if a parent has the time and patience, since head-banging usually stops when the child is held or distracted.

If a child bangs his head to get attention, or to get his way, then it is a bit more troublesome. Unless it is stopped, the child will continue to broaden his repertoire, using it to get all kinds of things (a cookie, a toy, mommy to play, etc.) or to get out of things (cleaning up, getting dressed, going to bed, taking medicine, etc.). It occurs most often after 18 months of age, though it can begin earlier. It must be stopped, and the sooner the better; left unchecked, it will escalate and be "used" in more and more situations, with ever-increasing severity, to eventually manipulate anyone and everyone possible.

How can you tell if it's manipulative? There are several telling signs. If it occurs as part of a tantrum – it is accompanied by whining, kicking, flailing, yelling – it is usually manipulative. If you know the child wants something – a toy, food, etc. – it is manipulative. If it occurs only when you leave the room (and he doesn't want you to), when an enjoyable activity is interrupted, or when he can't have something he wants, then it is manipulative. If it escalates – becomes more intense, with louder choruses of screaming, crying, or stomping – until he gets his way, it is manipulative. (Remember, self-stimulatory forms do not escalate – they are repetitive, calm, rhythmical, mild – and they are not accompanied by whining, screaming, or tantrums.)

It is not uncommon for children to try some form of self-abuse to get their way, even after two years of age. It's usually quite temporary if we handle it properly, but it can be scary. One child, at about three years of age, began to slam his head backward, against anything. At first, it was against the sofa, and we thought it might be just a form of play or rough-housing. But then he did it against the wall, the floor, and against his father's chin while sitting in his lap. He did it when he was mad, frustrated, or wanted mommy or daddy to play.

Studies investigating how to handle this kind of behavior all emphasize the same principles. First, the potentially injurious behavior cannot be allowed to "work," to get the child's way. Second, the child must be taught other, more appropriate ways of obtaining what he wants. Third, we must make a special effort to enrich the child's activities *when he's not doing this* – by playing with him; providing new games, toys, or stories; being accessible to him; doing enjoyable things together. These, if done *consistently*, will eliminate this behavior in most children. In those few instances in which this is not enough, researchers have added punishment to the plan, successfully (but more on that in a minute). First, let's go through these three procedures for dealing with self-injury in a bit more detail.

It is essential that a child who hits his head or bites his arm learns that nothing good will come of it. If you give in ("Oh, all right, I'll get you the toy this time.") to end his rage, the child learns that this is an effective way to get whatever he wants. Each time we give in, it strengthens and reinforces the behavior, and makes it much more difficult to treat later on. So if the child is hungry, delay giving food until the child has settled down for five to ten minutes; if he wants a toy, make sure he doesn't get it for now. In addition, it is no time for a discussion, explanation, or any other interaction with the child; after all, attention alone can be a big motivator for the child, and he will continue to head-bang just to get that attention.

As we discussed earlier (Parts 1 and 3), it is valuable to notice *why* the child is doing this, because it will help us get rid of the behavior. Does he want a cookie, daddy to play, watch a show on TV, play with a toy? If so, teach him an appropriate way to ask for or request it; that is, *we teach an appropriate alternative to head-banging*. Don't do it immediately after a head-banging or biting episode (or he may learn that biting eventually leads to getting what he wants); do it 15 minutes later, or whenever that self-injurious incident is clearly over and done with. Take him over to the toy he wanted, and ask him to say "toy, please" or have him just point to the toy. If necessary, demonstrate for him what you mean (how to do it). When he does this, give him the toy. Do the same thing for "cookie," "TV," "play," "outside," etc. Do each of these every day for several days. The purpose of course is to teach him different ways of expressing his wishes, and while teaching these we must let them be successful (we give him what he wants when he asks nicely). As he becomes successful at using these gestures and words, and when he uses them spontaneously and in a variety of situations, then we no longer have to give him what he wants all the time. For example, if it's before dinner, you may not want to give him a cookie – so you say, "OK, after dinner." Now, his communication still "works" most of the time. On occasion it doesn't, and most children can live quite happily with such a richly rewarding strategy (i.e. talking and gestures). *And it will be in stark contrast to self-injurious behavior, which never gets him what he wants.*

The third important aspect in this program is to enrich the child's activities when he is not self-injurious. This is helpful for several reasons. First, if we play together, and there's lots of enjoyable things to do, it will be a major loss when this is abruptly stopped (after an episode of self-abuse). It will make self-injury more negative, more unappealing, because the fun times disappear, immediately, whenever hitting, head-banging, biting, scratching, or hair-pulling occurs. In addition, if we are playing together and there is lots to do, there will be less reason to engage in head-banging. If he has engaging things to do most of the time – friends to play with, toys, things to do in the yard, parents who spend some "quality time" with him each day – his life will be rich, he'll be better able to handle not getting his way on occasion, and there will be less use for tantrums and self-injurious acts.

In the rare cases where a child might actually hurt himself, or the above techniques are not by themselves sufficient to entirely eliminate the self-abuse, various authors have added a negative consequence for the self-abusive act. We have already discussed in detail the right and wrong ways to use punishment (pages 45-52), and the reader should review that section carefully. For example, a sharp reprimand might be used – suddenly grabbing the child by both arms (startling him), lifting him quickly and abruptly toward you so your face is very close to his, making direct eye contact, together with a sharp, firm "No" – or a sharp slap on the hand, in the case of hand-biting or self-hitting.

When to get some help

If self-injury does persist past two years of age, or you are considering punishment, I would heartily recommend that you consult a psychologist. He or she can at least discuss your program and problem, reassuring you that you are doing the right thing – or can correct any misconceptions and provide additional guidance, supervision, and advice along the way. Psychologists are not there to stigmatize you or your child; they are there to assist you. I would be sure to ask for someone who specializes in children and is particularly experienced in self-injurious behavior.

Noncompliance and oppositional behavior

I can't imagine anything that upsets a parent more than trying to get compliance in a distracted or oppositional child – "Johnny, wait for me please . . . Honey? . . . Johnny? . . . Johnny, wait for me . . . Johnny, wait right there! . . . JOHNNY, stop this minute! . . . COME HERE RIGHT NOW!!!" By the third command or so, mom's walk has gotten brisker, her jaw is tense, and she's about to lose her groceries. By the fifth or sixth command, she breaks into a full gallop after her child, groceries flying everywhere, teeth grinding, completely embarrassed, muttering under her breath: "This time I'm really gonna KILL him." Sound familiar? Of course it does, because it happens to all of us. It is a normal (but unacceptable) child behavior; and childhood is just full of behaviors that are both normal and unacceptable (see the sections on aggression, tantrums, sleeping, fears, toileting, self-injury, etc.).

Compliance is number one on the "most wanted" list of parents. Fully one-third of all parental complaints – including all of the possible parental concerns discussed in this book – are about noncompliance in their children. Chances are very good that, at some point, it will be a concern of yours too.

Children's noncompliance is quite natural and normal – it occurs in virtually every child. After all, they're just learning that they can "move" people. As they learn that they can have an effect on people, they will naturally use their new-found skills more and more, exploring the range of possibilities and the limits of their influence. Kids will test the water, see how far they can go, and try to exert control over the world around them and the people in it.

While noncompliance is inevitable, we should of course not get carried away with it. This simply means that we should want and expect compliance *most* of the time. On the other hand, while we must be able to ensure a certain measure of compliance in our children, this too can be overdone – a child can become overly compliant, obeying the instructions of anyone and everyone (i.e. strangers), or a child may become unable to disobey even in the face of unreasonable demands (i.e. from peers). In short, we shouldn't get extreme in either direction – a certain amount of noncompliance must be tolerated, yet a parent must be able to get compliance when it is needed.

Definition
At first blush, a definition seems simple – compliance means that a child does what is asked of him, and noncompliance means

that he doesn't. It gets a bit more complicated, however. First, we want our child to do it (start) within a reasonable period of time – ten to 20 seconds, not two hours later. Second, we would prefer to have to ask only once (most parents start laughing about here, but read on). Third, some parents expect compliance to all manner of requests, demands, questions, suggestions, and other instructions – this would be unwise, however. We should expect full (100 percent) compliance only to demands: we wouldn't make it a demand unless it was very important, and it's crucial to know that we can get the child to obey when we need to. Then, we can let some noncompliance (free choice) occur in the case of suggestions ("Let's play with the blocks now."), questions ("Do you want to eat now?"), and requests ("Would you get my shoes for me, please.").

Consequently, our goal will *not* be for children to comply to all manner of requests, all the time – such excessive compliance is usually to serve the parents' whims, not the child's needs (and it may well do the child harm in preparing him for later years, as we'll see below).

A final note about definitions. We will not maintain a distinction between noncompliance and oppositional behavior because they are in fact very similar, and are dealt with in exactly the same way. The only real difference is that noncompliance implies that a child did not do what was asked, while oppositional behavior is a bit more extreme, as the child not only doesn't comply, but he may bite you on the nose, or do the opposite of what you asked. Oppositional behavior is considered a somewhat more severe form of noncompliance.

The incidence of compliance in normal children
Studies show that the normal rate of compliance is 60-80 percent (and therefore *non*compliance is 20-40 percent). Moreover, no differences have been found for boys versus girls, and no differences have been found in compliance to mothers versus fathers. Compliance does (should) increase further after age five, to the point at which noncompliance is no longer a concern.

While levels of compliance in the first three years of life have not proven to be very revealing about later years, compliance in the three-to-six age range has been found to be correlated with compliance later (in the six-to-fourteen age range). Consequently, excessive levels of noncompliance in the three-to-six age group seem to suggest noncompliance problems (i.e. disobedience, oppositional behavior, aggression, etc.) during later years.

Finally, studies have shown a clear relationship between noncompliance and other problem behavior. For example, excessive noncompliance in children has been associated with destructive behavior, crying, and tantrums.

Common parental reactions to compliance and noncompliance

As a rule, parents don't praise children when they are compliant. The average parent only praises compliance about 30 percent of the time. Some parents just "expect" compliance from their children, and don't feel it is deserving of any special praise. Others don't "notice" compliance among all the daily interactions with their child, or simply don't think of praising it. In most cases, compliance will improve, eventually, despite the absence of praise for it; in some, as we'll see, parents will have to praise it more. In all families, however, praising compliance more frequently will help to minimize noncompliance and oppositional behavior.

About one-third of the time, parents do not even give a child a chance to comply, as they verbally or physically help the child immediately, or within seconds of the instruction. This is a mistake, as it teaches the child that someone (guess who) will do it for him.

Some parents use yelling, threats, anger, humiliation, and nagging, along with demands, in an attempt to get compliance. Moreover, these parents may in general give an excessive number of demands to the child. This may serve to escalate the child's noncompliance into an even more negative and coercive reaction.

Finally, we find that parents are often much more tolerant of noncompliance up to the age of five. Beginning at the age of five, however, parents for some reason become a bit stricter – perhaps because this is the age when kids go to public school where more and more complex demands will be placed on the child, and parents want the child to do well in school (both in terms of socializing with other children, and in making a good impression on the teacher). Nothing will turn off a teacher and playmates faster than a noncompliant, uncooperative child.

With all this said, one wonders why children are compliant at all. It certainly does not seem to gain much respect, attention, or praise from mom and dad; and disobedience is usually put up with, or else it gets the child some help (parents do it for him).

The answer is simple. In most children, there are numerous other kinds of interaction between parents and children. Taking them all together, children usually learn that it is valuable or important to listen, and parents in a general sense do appreciate and attend to the accomplishments of their children. Parents come to have value and meaning to a child beginning on day one when mommy feeds the hungry baby. Children get things they want – food, toys, praise, outings, friends to visit – through their parents; they learn this quickly and rely heavily on their parents. Moreover, they also learn it is not good to get parents angry, upset, or otherwise disgruntled. These things are usually learned in sort of a general, unsystematic way – just by the natural way parents tend to and care for their children. One result is that children will usually listen and co-operate.

It is only when noncompliance occurs too often or lasts too long, that we may consider changing the "natural" way parents react to it.

Why are children noncompliant?
There are three basic reasons why children don't comply. First, if they like what they're already doing, they will not want to change or interrupt it. An example would be telling a child it's time for school or lunch, when he's happily playing with a friend. A second reason is that the child may not like what you're asking him to do: going to the doctor or dentist, bathing, putting things away, going to bed, taking medicine, are very common examples of requests that children often do not want to comply with. Finally, the third reason for noncompliance is to get a

reaction, a "rise" out of mom or dad . . . to watch your eyes grow bigger and listen to your teeth grind, to watch you get upset, flustered, and flabbergasted. It may also get the child a lot of personal attention and discussion.

It is of course inevitable that a child will be noncompliant at times. If she's happily playing with her toys, it can be downright maddening when a parent says, "It's time to eat now, let's go to the table." It's absolutely natural for a child to ignore it and see what will happen, to beg for "a few more minutes," to say, "No, I want to play," or to be carried into the kitchen kicking, crying, and screaming. After all, right now she'd rather play than eat. And while she may not invoke a constitutional right to the pursuit of happiness, that pursuit is wired into each of us, and we all explore ways to maximize fun and happiness.

Noncompliance is one strategy to get it – no more, no less. If it works, it will be used more often, and expanded to include a larger arsenal of tantrums, yelling, kicking, crying, begging, turning "limp," and (gulp), worst of all, "reasons" not to comply: "I'm not hungry," "I ate lunch already," "Billy hits me at school," "I can't go out in the sun because it makes me sad." These "reasons" may make us hesitate and wonder if we are doing the right thing (Jeez, did he already eat something? . . . did he have a late breakfast? . . . what if he's really not hungry? . . . does the sun really bother him?"). So, don't be surprised if your children try noncompliance; it would be surprising if they didn't.

Of major concern, however, is what a very astute researcher in Oregon calls the "coercive trap." Dr. Gerald Patterson has shown us that children learn to become more oppositional, destructive, and negative in order to stop or remove the parent's command. A parent may in turn become more coercive, threatening, and yell even louder to turn off the child's negative reaction. Then, the child may get even louder and more destructive to eliminate the parent's negative reaction. It can quickly and easily escalate into a verbal and/or physical free-for-all. To compound the situation, if a parent "gives in," then the child quickly learns that if he perseveres, gets more demanding, even violent, he will win. Parents can easily fall into this "trap" – it's a no-win situation that needs to be changed immediately!

In short, noncompliance is as normal as having children. It is to be expected in each of its many forms, and with its many associated behaviors (opposition, negativism, crying, kicking, tantrums, etc.). What is important is not whether it occurs, but how long the child continues it as a (successful) strategy for getting his or her way.

When is it a real problem?

For the first two years or so, I wouldn't even worry about it. Between the ages of three to six, however, noncompliance can be a bit more troublesome. The child likes to have his way, is used to having his way, and may even get a rise out of the reaction and attention he gets from noncompliance.

There are two situations where noncompliance is clearly a problem in the three-to-six-year-old. First, compliance normally occurs in children 60-80 percent of the time, so if compliance occurs much less than that, you should do something about it (and I'm sure you'll want to as it'll be driving you up the wall). Second, we should be able to ensure compliance to our *demands*, as opposed to our milder requests, questions, and suggestions: if a child does not listen in times of urgency or danger, we must teach him to.

Teaching compliance

In general, we're going to teach three things: first, that *compliance* is appreciated and richly rewarded with praise; second, that noncompliance does not pay; and third, if a *demand* is given, it must be complied with all of the time. In addition, we'll look at our own behavior. We'll reserve demands for when it is really important, and use milder requests, questions, and suggestions the rest of the time – and we'll not request excessive compliance to such requests and questions.

First, we must take a close look at our demands or instructions. Are we making too many – a constant barrage? Are we making some that we really don't mean, and some where we don't care that much if the child complies? Are we saying a lot of negative things – acting angry, posturing, nagging, and repeating demands over and over? If so, we simply eliminate all of it! You won't need it, and it doesn't help anyway. In short, don't make demands unless they are important and you mean to follow through. If you don't really care whether the child complies, then it should be offered in the form of a question, not a demand (i.e. "Would you like to eat now?" instead of "Go to the table and eat"; "Would you like to go outside?" instead of "Put on your jacket and go outside.") and let the child say (choose) "Yes" or "No."

Now that we've pared down our demands, we will say it only once. We will, however, look for ways to give a child some choice whenever we can. Giving him a choice seems to help as it "fades in" the demand, it prepares the child for a coming change in activities, rather than abruptly saying "It's time for dinner" right out of the blue. We might say, "Do you want to go to bed (eat, go to the store) now, or in five minutes? OK, then, we will go to bed (eat, leave) at 9:00" (on the digital clock, of course). When it is nine o'clock, the child is instructed, "It's 9:00, it's time to go to bed."

If the child does not comply, we give one (and only one) warning, "If you don't go to bed now, there will be no bedtime story. Now, I'm going to count to three. 1-2-3." If the child has not stopped what he is doing and *started* toward the bedroom by the time you hit "3," he is carried up to bed – no discussion and no delay – and no story is read.

You will undoubtedly have to carry him up to bed kicking and screaming a few times, and then listen to the sorrowful crying, whining, and sobbing emanating from his bedroom. It can be heartbreaking to listen to the crying, but the instruction was in fact important to you (otherwise you shouldn't have given it as a demand).

There are several important components of this procedure. First, we gave a warning. The warning is important in order to gain *future* compliance without having to go through the crying, kicking, and screaming. It tells the child he must do it, or he will face your displeasure and end up doing it anyway. It tells him your displeasure is not to be taken lightly. After a few occasions of carrying him through it, you will only have to start counting ("1 . . . 2") and the child will begin the new task at hand.

A second important part of this scenario is physically carrying the child upstairs (follow-through). This is essential, because it teaches him that no oppositional behavior will delay or prevent it from happening. If it's time to go to school, we get the jacket and put it on him and lead him by the hand (or carry him if necessary) to the car. If it's time to eat, he is taken to the table and remains there until he has at least eaten something (how much may vary – kids may lose their appetites when they're upset, but still must eat at least one bite so they understand that oppositional behavior will not serve to get them out of it).

A third component in this example is telling the child that you won't read a story to him if he doesn't go to bed. In short, there is some cost to being noncompliant. But it must be a *real* cost. If reading stories is not a normal part of your child's bedtime routine, or is not a particularly valued activity, then this is no great loss to the child. In that case, there must be some other cost of noncompliance. We can say that he won't get to sleep with (his favorite) brown bear, Barbie or He-Man doll; with his picture of Donald Duck, the Cookie Monster, or Raquel Welch on the wall; or, if necessary, we can take away something (pennies, toys). This does not mean we take away his security blanket – whether it be a blanket, diaper, or bear – but rather, we take away favorite toys and games, etc.

Other forms of noncompliance are dealt with in a similar fashion. My son would empty box after box of toys on the floor, never bothering to clean up one mess before he made another. We started requesting that he clean up one toy or game (i.e. Duplo or Leggo) before he played with another (i.e. the *Sesame Street* characters). Obviously, we weren't going to say that he wouldn't get a story at night – that was too delayed, too far away – we needed something for now. We simply said, "If you don't clean up the blocks first, you can't play with Bert and Ernie." Again, we had to go through it once or twice (making him clean up the blocks by holding his hand in mine and putting each block into the box, and then taking all the toys away for ten minutes), until he learned we meant it.

When noncompliance occurs, it is no time to explain, comfort, or have a discussion – the child may like any extra attention brought about by noncompliance. You want him to discover that oppositional behavior does *not* lead to good things, in any way, shape, or form. The message will be clearest, and most quickly learned, if you do not play, talk, or otherwise do enjoyable or engaging things for a period of time (i.e. ten minutes) after the episode of noncompliance.

One final point about this method for dealing with noncompliance: we must make a very special effort to give the child a wagonload of praise and encouragement when she is co-operative. It's easy to say or think that "she should do it, so why do I have to make a big deal of it?" This attitude won't help, and it certainly won't change anything for the better. Even parents who do generally praise their child for the good things they do, don't realize how often they fail to notice. As noted earlier, most people only praise compliance about 30 percent of the time. If compliance is deemed to be a concern, then the *first* thing we do is to increase that praise very substantially, to 90-100 percent of the time. The reason is simple – we want the message to be as clear as possible. When the child complies, nice things should consistently happen, to both motivate the child and to clearly and consistently get your message across. And nothing helps a child learn faster than picking her up, giving her a bear-hug, and saying "Oh-h, I'm so proud of you," not to mention just playing, reading or talking with her.

Overcompliance

While noncompliance is worrisome to many parents, we must be careful to separate the compliance necessary for the health and welfare of a child, versus compliance for compliance sake. Sometimes, we ask children to do things that are really not that important, or just a convenience to us: "Let's play with the blocks now"; "Will you throw this in the trash for me?" "Bring me a glass of water, OK?" To demand compliance to every whim, question, and request would be to do the child a disservice. The dangers to his future are several.

First, if a child becomes overcompliant, he often thinks compliance is a good thing everywhere. He may well comply to the requests of strangers, peers, etc., something no parent wants to see. He may become submissive and subservient to everyone.

In addition to being overcompliant to many people, the child may well be compliant to unreasonable requests. Playmates can make ludicrous requests, and often do, but most children don't just give away their toys, or accept arm-twisting without doing something back. The overcompliant child may.

If everyone was 100 percent compliant, who would have stood up for civil rights, sexual abuse of children, women's suffrage, prohibition, the ending of the Vietnam war, and so on. Our very lives, and the future of society, depend upon people's *judgments* of right versus wrong, and "100 percent compliance" clearly interferes with and prevents such judgment. Examples are not hard to find, such as the conformity and compliance of otherwise normal, everyday people in Nazi Germany. A bit closer to home, the very controversial research of Stanley Milgram, at Stanford University in the 1960s, showed that American college students complied when instructed to repeatedly shock another student (actually an actor), and even turned the level of the electric shock up past the "danger" point simply because they were told to do so by a man in a white laboratory coat. Many continued to do this even when they could see the victim pleading, in pain, writhing in agony, and crying.

While you may at first think these examples only marginally related to the topic at hand, they are very relevant. These examples illustrate that overcompliance is just as much a problem as noncompliance – they are both unhealthy sides of the same coin. So what are we to do?

We use "demands" sparingly, but require compliance to all demands

There are at least two valuable principles to keep in mind. First, when compliance is really needed or thought to be important, we give firm, clear, and direct instructions or demands. It is our voice, posture, and facial expression that tell a child that we "really mean it," that it is a demand. Noncompliance to these are simply not permitted, *ever*. When compliance is demanded, we can often explain why it is important – in this way the child can learn the "rules" about when compliance is to be required, and parents are forced to think through (and evaluate) their reasons for demanding compliance in each situation. We do not, however, use demands, or *require* compliance, for activities that are arbitrary, or a convenience for the parent; here we do not use a firm voice, and may even word it as a question. If a question is used, the answer is up to the child – compliance (your preferred answer) is not required.

Second, we teach the child, as she gets older (it can begin even at four years of age) about noncompliance, when it is called for, simple lessons of history. This of course requires judgments of fairness, right and wrong, helping others, safety, and reasonable and unreasonable requests. We use lots of examples of when to comply *and* when not to comply, together, so the child can see the *differences* between the two situations (i.e. if your uncle offers you a ride home, it's OK; if you don't know the person, run away).

Toilet training

There are three typical concerns parents have about toileting: 1) initially teaching the child how to use the toilet rather than wet her pants or diaper; 2) soiling ("encopresis"); and 3) bed-wetting ("enuresis"). Virtually all parents will have to tackle each of these. Moreover, I have seen many children become fascinated with bowel movements and genitals during toilet training, so don't be surprised to see other kinds of "problems", such as a bowel movement used as a missile, a gift, or for finger painting or other artistic expression.

While parents do want their child to learn proper toileting skills, we don't have to worry about any psychological problems or maladjustment – after all, it won't be a concern when he's six or seven. We can relax a bit, realize it's primarily a matter of convenience when we train the child, and how early or urgently we want her to stay dry.

This is not to make light of that convenience. After two or three years of changing diapers and pants, it can get very, very old. In fact, when there is disagreement between parents about when to do toilet training, it is usually the father who doesn't see any pressing concern. This is easily resolved, however, by having the father take over the diaper-changing.

Some parents feel that toilet training is related to intelligence – the child who can be toilet-trained early must be especially bright. In fact, intelligence has little to do with toilet training – if a child meets the developmental readiness test described below, he can be trained; if not, he can't. It's as simple as that. Furthermore, just because a child is ready for training does not mean it is the best or only time to do it. Many parents think they must do training the instant the child is prepared to receive it, or as early as possible. This is not the case. Toilet training gets easier to do as the child gets older, and when you should do it is primarily a matter of convenience (within limits of course, but they are wide limits).

Fortunately, all of these toileting "problems" can be dealt with, often rather simply and quickly, with a little planning. According to the research, toilet training can be successfully accomplished in up to 95 percent of children by the age of three, and often earlier.

Incidence and norms

The very large majority of children have stopped soiling and (daytime) wetting by the age of five. This means that parents, left to their own resources, get the job done quite nicely, thank you. Most children can, however, be taught to use the toilet at two years of age, and some as early as 18 months; if you are anxious to start toilet training this early, you may need a little assistance (described below) because the baby is so immature.

These ages are just averages, however, and may not apply to your child. The true test of whether or not a child is ready for toilet training has nothing to do with age, but rather depends on certain specific readiness skills and maturation (described below).

Bed-wetting, on the other hand, is often a bit more difficult for children, and it may continue even after toilet training is mastered; bed-wetting occurs in about 15 percent of children over the age of five, but it, too, can be easily and effectively dealt with in over 80 percent of bed-wetters.

When is a child ready for toilet training?

The literature suggest four simple tests for readiness:

1) *Bladder control.* First, a child should urinate a fair amount at one time, rather than small amounts more often during the day. Second, the child should stay dry for several hours at a time. Third, in most (but not all) children you should be able to tell when they have to go by their facial expressions (grimacing), body movements (rocking the pelvis, unable to sit still), or special postures (bent over a bit, standing unusually still, and tensing the rear end). If these three occur, we can be confident that the child recognizes the proper bladder signs and sensations.

2) *Physical Maturation.* Can the child walk easily from room to room? Does he have enough motor control to pull down his pants? If so, he is physically ready.

3) *Language Development.* The child should be able to understand simple concepts that will be needed during training – she should understand "up," "down," "potty," "arms," "legs," "wet," "dry," etc., and be able to imitate simple things you do (pull pants down, etc.).

4) *Compliance.* Does the child usually listen to you and follow through on your instructions, or is she often stubborn and noncompliant?

If a child passes all four tests, he is ready for toilet training. If bladder control, physical maturation, or language development are insufficient, we can simply wait until they develop. If noncompliance is a problem, however, we shouldn't depend on just the passage of time to solve it. Rather, we use the principles and procedures outlined for noncompliance (pages 118-127). We do this separately, and before we even begin toilet training, because we do not want toileting to become associated with noncompliance (or "battles" to get compliance), tantrums, upsets, or fears.

Urination training

The literature shows several procedures which are highly effective in teaching children to urinate in the toilet. If they are used consistently and diligently, a child can be taught to go to the toilet (or potty), pull down her pants, urinate, flush, and pull up her pants. The quickest results are achieved if you devote some time solely to your child and the toilet training, ignoring *all* distractions (a doorbell, phone, preparing meals, etc.). If you are unable to be so concentrated about it, it will take a bit longer – perhaps a few weeks. The principles are as follows:

1) We conduct *frequent checks* of the child's diaper – every five minutes or so for fastest results – until the child has some success in the potty. This means we simply look in or feel the diaper to see if it is dry. We do this wherever the child happens to be – eating in the kitchen, watching TV in the den, playing in the living room or bedroom.

2) We use *lots of approval and praise* whenever a diaper-check reveals a dry diaper. In addition, we praise the child for standing (boys) or sitting (girls) at the potty when we tell them to go there, for *trying* to urinate while at the potty, and, of course, for actual urination in the potty.

3) We model or *demonstrate* for the child. Either a parent can ask the child to go to the toilet with them, showing them how, or a doll can be used (in fact, dolls that wet are readily available). Each time we go, we demonstrate, and then prompt or help as necessary, showing the child how to pull down his pants, sit on the toilet, pull up his pants, flush the toilet, and wash his hands.

4) When the child is on the toilet, we talk, play, listen to music, read stories, etc., so that it is a comfortable, *relaxed place* to be.

5) We *never use spankings, yelling, or anger* for accidents, because we do not want toileting to become associated with upsets, fear, incontinence, and the like.

6) We *voice our displeasure* at accidents, matter-of-factly, not angrily – "I'm disappointed you wet your diaper instead of going in the toilet."

7) When accidents occur, we have *the child* clean up (to the best of his ability), change clothes, and practise going to the toilet. Cleaning up should not be a pleasant tête-à-tête; it should involve little discussion with you, yet help the child to do it if he's too young to do it on his own.

8) We *watch for any indication that a child needs to go* (those signs of bladder control – grimacing, posturing, pelvis rocking, etc.), and quickly instruct the child to go to the potty (or toilet), helping him if necessary.

9) We *take the child to the potty regularly*, every 15 minutes or so, stay with her, and ensure that it is a relaxed, comfortable atmosphere. We stay for about ten minutes – if she goes in the potty, the child is richly praised; if not, the child pulls up her pants and leaves the potty. After 15 minutes, we return again. Each time she goes to the potty, she practices pulling her pants down, sitting (or standing) at the potty, pulling her pants up, flushing, etc.

10) We give the child *lots of liquids*, using his favorites (this should not be forced) so he will willingly drink – sodas, juices, milk, etc. This will provide more opportunities for urination, more practice and success, and quicker learning.

11) We always *explain* – we use the words "dry" and "wet" when we are praising or voicing our displeasure, so the child will understand what led to it, what it means, which is desirable and undesirable.

All this should be a *positive experience* for the child – ensured by lots of praise and attention. The only time the child may get a bit upset might be when he is required to clean up after accidents – but even this is minor and nothing to worry about if a

parent is generous with attention and praise for trying, sitting on
the potty, and any successes the child has.

Soiling

Soiling is dealt with in virtually the same manner as urination. In
fact, it can be done at the same time, in which case a "dry"
diaper means that the child has neither soiled nor wet. This may
of course require a little extra training time.

Bed-wetting

Bed-wetting is due primarily to the fact that children often don't
attend to bladder signs when they are asleep. Bed-wetting is,
however, relatively simple to treat, but it should not be at-
tempted until daytime toileting has been successfully mastered –
it is important that we know the child has the proper toileting
routines down pat before worrying about nighttime wetting.

Special mattress pads and training pants have been developed
to sound a buzzer when wetness from urination causes a small
circuit to close. These have long been popular in the treatment of
bed-wetting, for good reason. They have been widely used and
studied since the 1930s; they are absolutely safe; they are easy to
use; and most of all, they are very effective, successfully
eliminating bed-wetting in 80-90 percent of all cases. They are
both readily available to the public.

When a child wets the bed, a buzzer sounds and a parent
wakes the child, takes him to the bathroom, and requires him to
change his pajamas. Usually nothing more is needed, since the
child has already learned how to get to the toilet and what to do
there; in fact, he is usually proud that "I can do it myself," and
only needs to learn to react to those same bladder signs at
nighttime.

This procedure is not reserved (as many parents seem to think)
for a "severe" bed-wetter – it is totally benign (safe and harm-
less), comfortable for the child, and appropriate for any child
who wets the bed. A parent need not wait until the child is eight
or ten years of age, letting him become terribly self-conscious
and concerned about the situation over the years.

A final important point about bed-wetting. It is *not deliberate,* and there is no reason whatsoever to shame, punish, or reprimand the child. Such punishment can only hurt the child in this case, because it does not teach him how to do it properly. Also, the child may well be trying, and he will feel punished despite trying his best – something we *never* want to do. I know of many parents who try to threaten, spank, shame, or embarrass a child into staying dry – these tactics are not only useless but harmful, for the child simply doesn't know how to attend to the bladder signs while he is sleeping. The buzzer-pad approach is simple, effective, and *teaches* a child to react (awaken) to those bladder signals during the night.

Sleeping problems

P utting a child to bed can be a very tough row to hoe. Beginning around 18-24 months, most children simply do not like (they hate) going to bed – there are toys to be played with, people to see, worlds to conquer. I have never met a parent who didn't struggle with the question of what to do about it – should I let him cry until he falls asleep, comfort and sit with him until he falls asleep, take him into my bed? And Lord above, listening to a baby cry himself to sleep can be like a dagger twisting and turning in the pit of your stomach: the guilt ("Am I doing the right thing?") can be intense. To prevent guilt, and children's tears, parents often develop elaborate bedtime routines – songs, stories, games, food, and drink – lasting as long as two to three hours, including staying with the child until she falls asleep. The hope is, of course, that eventually the routine will get shorter. But it often doesn't . . . until we tackle the problem head on. Somehow, eventually, the child must learn to go to sleep without a parent being present, instead of only falling asleep with a parent in hand.

While putting a child to bed is without question the most common concern about sleeping in children, others include disruptive sleep (waking frequently), nightmares, night terrors, and sleepwalking. None of these, however, are associated with any type of emotional problem in children; to the contrary, sleeping difficulties are quite normal and common, and children do usually grow out of them. Even so, it can be a trying time for both children and parents, and much is learned by the child during this time, about nighttime and darkness, compliance, the relative effects of pleading and throwing a tantrum, not to mention the quality of room service.

Norms in sleeping time and sleeping routines

When a child comes home from the hospital, she's usually sleeping about 16 hours per day. She continues to sleep 15-16 hours per day for the first three to four months, after which it gradually and steadily declines to about 11 hours per day at six years of age. Table 4-4 shows the average sleep-time for young children at different ages.

In addition, the average *longest sleep* during the day is four hours for a one-week-old infant, which increases to 8.5 hours at 15 weeks (Table 4-4) – so the difficult task of getting up at all hours to tend to the baby may begin to ease noticeably sometime after 15 weeks. On average, the longest *waking period* during the day is two and a half hours at one week of age, which increases steadily to 3.6 hours at 15 weeks of age – as the child gets older she is awake for longer periods of time (she takes fewer naps).

For any given child, however, sleeptime may vary. In general, I would not worry about a baby's sleeptime unless it varies consistently and substantially from these norms. Even if your baby does require more or less sleep, that does not mean there is a problem – but I would check with a doctor if a baby's sleeptime varied from this table by more than two hours on a regular basis.

In terms of nightly routines, the time to go to bed varies dramatically in different families. Some parents prefer a set bedtime, so they can have time alone or time to finish other tasks. Other parents wait until their child is tired each night before putting him to bed, in which case bedtime may vary from day to day, from 6:30 to 10:30 (or later). The choice is simply up to you, as most children can easily adapt to either type of schedule. The length of the bedtime routine – talking, reading a story, playing a game – should last for 15-30 minutes on average.

Table 4-4

Average sleeping and waking time for babies and young children:

Age	Hours of daily sleep	Hours awake per day	Longest sleep (hours)	Longest waking period (hours)
1 week	16.3	7.7	4.4	2.6
3 weeks	15.4	8.6	4.6	3.1
7 weeks	15.4	8.6	6.5	3.2
11 weeks	15.1	8.9	7.7	3.4
15 weeks	14.9	9.1	8.5	3.6
6 months	13.2	10.8		
7-9 months	12.7	11.3		
10-12 months	11.8	12.2		
2-3 years	12.5	11.5		
3-4 years	11.5	12.5		
4-6 years	11.0	13.0		

Definition and incidence of various sleeping difficulties

Difficulties in *going to bed* cover a wide range of activities, all revolving around the notion that a child won't go to sleep on his own. Some children stay up until all hours, eventually falling asleep near their toys, in front of the TV, or on the sofa; some will only sleep with a parent nearby or only after long bedtime routines that last a couple of hours; some will only sleep in their parents' bed, or with a parent in their bed; some will ask endlessly for a drink of water, to go to the bathroom, for an apple or a cookie, in order to lure a parent back into the room; and some resist even starting the bedtime routine – refusing to put on their pajamas, take a bath, or go to the toilet. Beginning around 18-24 months, most parents will face such difficulties in putting their child to bed.

Waking problems, on the other hand, refer to a child waking at night after having been asleep for a while. Most people (adults and children) do wake briefly at night, but fall right back to sleep. It is only when a child cries or demands attention on a regular basis, instead of settling back to sleep, that this becomes a problem. This is not at all uncommon, and it decreases with age – about 20 percent of two-year-olds wake up their parents regularly at night, about 14 percent of three-year-olds, and 8 percent of four-year-olds. Usually, it requires no special treatment since the child is tired and, with some comforting, falls right back to sleep.

Sleepwalking is relatively rare, occurring in about six percent of children. Children who sleepwalk may actually go outside, climb out a window, or take a brief walk around the room, without even waking up. In fact, they are actually difficult to waken, even though their eyes may be open and they appear to have some goal or purpose in mind. This is only of concern if the child can place himself in some danger – by walking near a staircase, balcony, or climbing out an open window. Since he is not alert, and not functioning normally, he may not protect himself from a fall or from other types of accidents.

It is difficult to tell when children begin to have *nightmares*, but many believe they begin as early as the second year; they are, however, most common in three- to five-year-olds, and virtually all children seem to have some nightmares. Nightmares usually last only a few minutes and then the child wakes up. Typically, the child remembers things about the nightmare and can tell you something about it. *Night terrors*, on the other hand, are a bit different, and much scarier for a parent. The night terror can last 15-20 minutes and the child does not awaken, even though his eyes may be open and he has a scared expression on his face. Children's movements (i.e. writhing) and vocalizations (i.e. yelling) are much greater and more intense than those found in nightmares: the child is difficult to waken, and attempts at comforting the child have no effect. The cause of nightmares and night terrors are largely unknown. Fortunately, however, while nightmares are common, night terrors are very rare indeed – primarily occurring in children over five years of age, and then only in about two percent of children.

Why do children have these sleeping difficulties?
Children may have difficulty in *going to bed* for a variety of
reasons. The most common, of course, is that they would
prefer to do something else. A close second is that they hate
to be alone (especially in the dark or quiet isolation of a bedroom). In addition, the child may be very excited, active or
aroused, and it may be difficult for him to settle down for
bedtime. Another possibility is that a child simply isn't tired
– perhaps he slept in that morning, or had a nap after swimming with dad. Finally, a child may be afraid, upset perhaps
by the quiet or the dark, a frightening TV show or story, or an
unsettling event during the day.

Many parents have a lot of uncertainty and guilt about wanting their child to sleep on their own. They often worry that their
child will feel rejected and alone. This of course makes them
jump at every cry or whimper, as their feelings of love and devo-
tion for the child take priority over their own needs. What happens, of course, is that the child learns how to get the parent to
come-a-running. I've seen *so* many children who continue to say,
"I'm so-o-o sad," when they are not sad; "I'm afraid," when they
are not afraid; who cry or whine as soon as a parent leaves the
room; who ask for a drink, to go to the bathroom, or for food . . .
endlessly. Why? Because it worked before – when they were
really afraid, sad, hurt, or hungry, they got some company. Why
shouldn't it work now, even though they are not now afraid, sad,
hurt, or hungry? They can't know that mommy won't return at
nighttime, until and unless they find out that parents really
mean it when they leave and in fact they don't return. This will
be one approach to dealing with the problem, although many
positive aspects will be added to take much of the sting out of it.
More important, if parents know that they have given the child
ample time to go to the bathroom, eat, drink, chat, share a story,
and play together, before going to sleep, there is no reason to feel
guilty about saying goodnight and leaving her to fall asleep.

Nightmares may at times be related to frightening or upsetting
events during the day, yet often it just isn't clear what
precipitated a nightmare. It seems that they begin after a child
discovers "good guys" and "bad guys," monsters, and the like.

In a general sense they seem to occur when the child's imagination and creativity begin to emerge. In terms of *night terrors* and *sleepwalking*, we know very little about why they occur – there are many different theories, but none have been substantiated.

When are sleeping difficulties a real problem?

Rarely are any of these sleep patterns a real problem for the child – that is, they usually disappear with age. Even strategies for putting a child to bed, of concern to most parents, are not usually a lasting problem; child-rearing fads have swung from one extreme (strictness) to the other (permissiveness) over generations of parents, and children have not shown any apparent scars. In general, then, one need not be concerned about a child's emotional adjustment at these times – rather, we simply want to find some fair compromise that considers *both* the child's and the parent's needs. As long as we are not extreme – putting a child to bed in an abrupt fashion, ignoring real fears, etc. – the question rests on what a parent is able and comfortable in doing. Wanting time to yourself is neither a sin nor something to feel guilty about – it is a legitimate need. Reserving a little time for yourself is actually better *for the child*, if it allows you to be more attentive to the child and less irritable during the time you are together.

There is another way in which bedtime routines can be a problem – it can be a problem *of* the parent, rather than *for* the parent. I've met many parents who actually prefer to sleep with their child – for their own sake, not for the child's – and continue to do so on a regular basis even when the child is five or six years old. There is absolutely nothing wrong with enjoying the comfort of your child next to you, or comforting him when he is afraid, but like any other behavior it can be a problem if it is carried to extremes. Fostering such dependency in children, or becoming overly dependent on them, may reflect fundamental emotional problems in the parent, or in the marriage: it may show an unhealthy overprotectiveness, or doting, on a parent's part. It has even been used as a contraceptive: to prevent sexual activities with a spouse by having a child in bed. I've also seen many cases of "musical beds," with one parent being unable to sleep due to overcrowding, a child's fidgeting, an accidental elbow to the head, or a foot in the ribs: that parent then moves to another bed (or sofa) in the middle of the night in order to get a decent night's sleep.

In general, if a bedtime routine *regularly* interferes with a parent's sleep, work, domestic chores, or sexual activity, it simply must be changed or else severe family problems will undoubtedly follow. Similarly, if a bedtime routine reflects a problem in the parent or marriage – the parent who is overly dependent on the child, or "using" the child to prevent sexual advances at night – then the real problem needs to be dealt with in a more healthy and constructive way, for all concerned.

How to handle sleeping problems

There are some principles that are very fundamental and basic to helping all of these sleeping difficulties.

1. It is valuable to have a bedtime routine. This does not mean that there can't be exceptions to it – on special occasions, when a friend sleeps over, when a child is afraid, during an illness – but there should be a routine nonetheless; one that is generally adhered to, so a child knows when bedtime is coming and can prepare for it.

2. The child must be awakened at a fairly regular time each morning. If a child sleeps in for a few hours (or takes a nap after soccer), we cannot expect him to go to sleep at the regular time that night. He simply won't be tired. We must be sure that a child is ready to go to sleep (i.e. is somewhat tired) before we put him to bed, and this requires us to coordinate the waking-time and the bedtime. On days when the child wakes substantially earlier or later – and of course such occasions will inevitably occur (illness, sleeping in, travel, and vacations, etc.) – the bedtime must be allowed to vary too.

3. We should let a child know five to 15 minutes ahead of time that bedtime is coming, so she can finish whatever she is doing.

4. The bedtime routine should include some relaxing, quieting activities, with a parent present and participating, before it's time to sleep. Reading stories, making up stories and songs, talking about the day's events, are common examples. This can last 15-20 minutes, or longer if a parent wishes.

5. One should also include in the bedtime routine any drinks or food permitted, as well as going to the bathroom, so that the child will have no reason to ask for these things immediately after going to bed – you'll know it's manipulative, rather than a real need to go to the bathroom.

6. Any comforters that may soothe or calm a child should be given – a favorite blanket, teddy bear, *Sesame Street* characters, Super-Heroes, etc.

7. Distractions should be removed wherever possible – loud music or TV should be toned down; a night-light can be used if necessary (but not the brighter overhead light); and children should have their own beds if possible, so they are less likely to wake each other up.

8. If parents are concerned about a child's resistance to going to bed, or about overly long bedtime routines, whatever changes are made to that routine must be agreed to by both parents: nothing will undermine your efforts faster than mom steeling herself to endure the child's crying until the child nods off to sleep, while the next night dad goes in to stay with the child at the first sign of a whimper.

While these eight points are basic to all children, and helpful for any of the sleeping difficulties we have described, there are some additional procedures specifically designed for each of the nighttime problems, as follows.

i. Putting a child to bed

The infant is used to falling asleep with you at hand, as she at first falls asleep in your arms after breast- or bottle-feeding. Sometime between 12-24 months, we will have to make a change. The major change we have to make is simply this: somehow he has to be put to bed *before he is asleep*. If we keep this goal in mind – leaving the room *before* he falls asleep – there are two general ways to go about it.

First, we can tell him it's time for bed, go through the bedtime routine, and then tuck him in (while he's awake), and leave the room. We can spice up the room (with special posters, stuffed animals, toys) so that the bedroom is a nice place to be; and we can spice up the bedtime routine (special hugs, stories, etc,) to make it as enjoyable as possible – but we must leave *before* he is asleep. At first, the child may resist your leaving, trying a range of things to get you back – crying, asking for things (water, bathroom, food, more water), etc. This can be very trying because of course the child is really sad and does want you to come back. We can ease the upset in a variety of ways; for example, putting teddy bears, comforters, and toys in the bed with the child. While some parents may not like the idea of having toys in bed, it is not a bad idea at first – it helps to distract a child while getting him used to the parent not being there. When the child is accustomed to falling asleep without the parent being there, *then* one can reduce the toys, if necessary, so he falls asleep faster.

We can go much further in trying to make the bedtime routine as enjoyable as possible. We can tell her there will be a "surprise" (i.e. an inexpensive toy) under her pillow in the morning if she goes to sleep without getting up. We can have some games, toys, stories, rhymes, or songs that are *only* available during the bedtime routine – and we can add to that lots of hugs, kisses, handholding, and talking – so that bedtime is in fact a very enjoyable and "special" time.

But we must leave the child's room while she is awake. If we do this, and don't return (except of course in an emergency, when there is an illness, or if the child has been asleep and then wakes up), the child will learn to fall asleep on her own. When the child realizes that you mean it – that you will not return – the upsets will disappear, and this usually takes only a week or so (the toughest part is the first two to three days). The anxiety of bedtime will dissipate, for both the parents and the child, and bedtime will improve 100 percent.

The second way to do this is similar, but more gradual. For the first few days, you may stay in the room, on her bed, *until the child is drowsy* – but you should close your eyes, not talk with the child, and pretend to go to sleep. For the next few days, you can sit in a chair and read, instead of lying on the bed or holding hands. You can then stay in the room for shorter and shorter periods of time. For example, if it takes an hour for her to get drowsy after the bedtime story, then I would begin to leave after 50 minutes over the next few days, then after 40 minutes for a few days, and so on, until you finally leave as soon as the bedtime stories are over.

ii. Waking during the night

If a child wakes in the night and calls out, I would go to him. As noted earlier, this is rarely a problem since the child is usually still tired, possibly afraid from a nightmare, and he easily falls back to sleep with a little comforting. This problem tends to decrease with age, so I wouldn't give it any special handling unless it happens several times per night, on a consistent basis, and appears to be manipulative. In those (rare) instances where it is a problem, a parent should go in only once each night (to make sure nothing is really wrong, like an illness or nightmare), explain to him that you must go back to sleep and will not return, and then leave *while he is still awake* so that he learns to go back to sleep on his own.

iii. Nightmares and night terrors

If the child wakes up afraid, we go to comfort her. We provide any and all comfort that can help to calm and relax the child. We may hold the child and rock her back to sleep, show there are no monsters under the bed, explain that dragons sleep at night, tell her that Big Bird, Barbie or He-Man is not afraid of those monsters and will protect her.

In addition to comforting the child, we try to give him ways to cope with and master the situation , so that he is not afraid. We may put his sword on the floor next to his bed, put the princess with magical powers on her dresser so that it protects her from any evil, place stuffed animals strategically around his room to protect him and catch any "bad guys," turn on the night-light since the evil one is afraid of the light, and so on.

Most of all, we just comfort the child, and stay until he is calm or goes back to sleep.

Making the bedtime routine fun for parents

Bedtime is a tough time for many parents. They're often tired from the long day, thinking about things still to be done, wanting some peace and quiet, or time to themselves. Bedtime can easily become an unpleasant routine, something we just want to get finished in order to be free. In fact, this can happen quite unknowingly, when bedtime becomes rote, perfunctory, a "going through the motions." The result of this, unfortunately, is more bedtime problems, a longer bedtime routine, since the child isn't going to like it either.

A real key to bedtime is to make it "quality time," a special time when we really tune in to our child. We can actually *look forward to it* if we include things we like to do in the bedtime routines. If we include things we and the child like to do, it will very naturally turn into a special time for all. There may be simple games you both like. (For example, an enjoyable memory game for many adults and four-year-olds: turn 12 playing cards face-down on the bed, including two Aces, Kings, Queens, Jacks, 10s and 9s – and use more or less cards if it's too easy or hard. Then try to find the matched pairs, with one person only getting to turn over two cards at a time; we take turns, and when we find a pair [turn over two identical cards on our turn], we keep the cards. Each person watches what the other person turns over, and tries to remember where they were. The person with the most cards at the end wins.) There are many games both parent and child can enjoy, if you take the time to look – and there are tons of books, lists, newsletters, etc. to guide you.

In addition, if we really talk to the child, ask questions, make up stories together ("What do you think Barbie did then?"), try to make her eager, attentive, or just smile – it will be special. You can make faces, gurgle strange noises, exaggerate your expressions and moods (show a "surprised face," a silly face, a mad face), ask questions about the pictures in the book, and find in the end that it's a lot of fun for both of you.

The bottom line is making the bedtime routine as enjoyable as possible for *both* the parents and their children. Parents will find that they notice things about their child, about their personality and development, that they hadn't noticed before; the children will feel special and enjoy this close, personal contact and attention. The bedtime routine will get shorter, as both parent and child part in a good mood and disruptions are minimized.

The relationship between bedtime difficulties and noncompliance

If a parent has used the compliance-teaching recommendations described in the noncompliance section, putting a child to bed will be much, much easier. If a child has already learned that a demand – as opposed to questions, gentler requests, and instructions – must be carried through all the time, it will help to make going to bed a piece of cake. If we have adopted these principles – giving demands rarely, only when they are important, and in a firm deliberate voice (and insisting each demand be carried through) – then a command to go to bed will be just another command, often not needing any special handling at all. If we are sparing in our use of demands – using questions or requests (in which case a child can do otherwise if he wishes) when it is not that important or just a minor inconvenience to us – then demands will continue to have meaning and they will be complied with. (It is important, however, not to demand that a child "go to sleep" – this can't be turned on and off like a light switch. Instead, we can say, "Put on your pajamas," or "Go to bed now," if demands are in fact needed.)

Aggression

Parents are often shocked when they first see aggression in their child: "Where the devil did that come from? – he HIT that child!"; "Honey, ya know what just happened? *Your* daughter got in a snit and *scratched* my face!"; "How dare you THROW that at me!"; "Can you believe our little princess just up and pushed that child off the swing? . . . I'm gonna kill her!" Moreover, a bright child may figure out when aggression is most likely to work – in public places, when you're tired (and easy prey) – and the child will come on like a whirlwind at those times. In fact, the literature shows that it is often the most competent, bright children who are most aggressive at the age of two to three – but the aggression declines over the next few years as appropriate (alternative) social and verbal skills develop.

Most children will display aggression at some time, in some form. One child may throw or destroy things; another may push, kick, or bully others; another may be verbally abusive, yelling, screaming, teasing, and demanding. While such aggression is quite normal in young children, it is true that aggression of a "severe" nature is associated with later adult problems. So it is not surprising that aggression is a major concern to most parents.

There are two issues that are important here for parents. First, we should know the difference between "normal" and "severe" aggression; and second, we should know how to react to the normal aggression so that it does not become severe.

Definition

In general, aggression is any behavior designed to hurt (physically or psychologically) another person. It can take many forms. The physically aggressive child may bully, hit, kick, push, spit, and assume various threatening postures (which are often exaggerated – the chin sticking out a mile, lips pursed, eyes squinting, legs spread, ready for battle). The verbally aggressive child may scream at the top of his lungs until he gets his way, not to mention being demanding, name-calling, or using threats; the destructive child may throw toys or dishes, smash things on the ground, stomp on them, kick them, or crash them into each other (and often these will occur in sequence, one after the other, until the room is practically demolished).

It is important, however, to distinguish between aggression and appropriate forms of assertiveness. Some assertiveness may well be important to future adjustment, happiness, and success. We want children (and adults) to be assertive rather than passive in the face of unjust demands; some competitiveness is woven into the very fabric of adolescence (school, grades, sports) and adult life (work); some ambition – striving to further oneself and improve our lot in life – is considered desirable. While aggression is not adaptive, such forms of assertiveness are in fact essential to coping with the demands of life.

Normal patterns and incidence of aggression

Aggression is not usually a concern until a child is at least two years of age, when it may be triggered by new toileting, eating, and sleeping routines, or other demands that are placed on a child. However, the literature reveals that aggressive episodes will then typically decrease with age. As the child continues to develop new social, verbal, and motor skills, he learns appropriate ways to request or obtain what he wants. The form or style of aggression also changes with age. While physical aggression may be dominant in a two-year-old, it decreases while verbal aggression increases as the child gets older; the six- to seven-year-old generally resorts to yelling, threatening, posturing, and name-calling, instead of hitting, kicking, and pushing. (Later, children are more inclined to sulk, hold grudges, and tease.)

It is notable that aggression problems rarely *begin* in adolescence; overly aggressive adults were almost always overly aggressive children. Don't misunderstand, though. This does *not* mean that all aggressive children become aggressive teenagers and adults – in fact, 70 percent of children who do have an aggression problem do *not* become aggressive teenagers or adults. Rather, the point is that if aggression is not a problem in childhood, it will not be a problem later in life.

Why are children aggressive?

The primary way children learn aggression is through modelling or imitation. They see others do it, and they try it. They may see it on TV, in peers, or in parents. Furthermore, being exposed to aggressive models not only teaches a child different ways to be aggressive, it also has a *disinhibiting* effect – he will be less inclined to stop or hold back the aggression.

A tremendous body of research concerning violence on TV has clearly shown that children imitate what their heroes do, even cartoon heroes, so don't be surprised if a child tries to fly, practise karate kicks, or pops someone on the nose who took his toy. Children also commonly adopt aggressive patterns of their parents – don't be surprised to see him swearing, teasing, nagging, yelling, if mommy or daddy do that. In fact, they'll often copy your very intonation, facial expressions, and postures – and exaggerate them (it can look funny, but if you have to laugh, go to the bathroom and do it; not in front of Junior). Even if they never see aggression in parents, and you have no TV, they will still see it in peers, imitate it, and try it.

We should of course try to prevent aggression – it is wise not to expose our children to too many violent models (new ways to be aggressive). We may try to limit their exposure to aggression by restricting the amount of TV-watching, by controlling the kinds of shows they may watch, which children they can play with, by not arguing in front of the children, and so on. But it is impossible to prevent all exposure to aggression; peers and schoolmates will show them if no one else does.

The truth is, however, that how children first learn aggression is not nearly as important as whether or not it is successful when it does occur. It will occur; it cannot be prevented. If it is often successful, they will continue it, expand it, elaborate it, try it in new and different situations, and use it against new and different people (peers, teachers, siblings, etc.).

Certain family interactions tend to foster and support aggression in children. For example, aggression is common in children when parents are too permissive and indulgent. Parents who cater to a child's every whim, indulge him, always "try to understand" tantrums and aggression – by talking, explaining, soothing the child, without ever resisting or dealing firmly with the aggression – are actually teaching the child that aggression will get him what he wants. Aggression will flourish in such a richly rewarding environment. As the old saying goes, the indulgent parent lets him get away with murder, and murder he will do to get his way.

Unnecessary and excessive use of spanking, verbal abuse, rejection, nagging, and punitiveness, can also foster and support aggression in children. The parents are essentially modelling for the child what they think is the right way to change another person's behavior; they are implicitly giving him permission to do it too, and he very probably will (though not necessarily to the parents).

In some families, parents take out their frustrations about work, bills, etc., on the family. The child of course thinks he did something wrong, but can't figure out what it could be. If this pattern continues, the child may become quite sad, enraged, depressed, and of course aggressive. Moreover, if that parent fails to praise the good things that children (and others) do, negative interactions and punishment really dominate the scene. The child will copy such negative actions. In fact, the child may try to yell louder, stomp more, generally blow a gasket just to get that parent's attention, or perhaps to stop the parent from nagging or yelling at him. And it easily and quickly becomes a vicious cycle, as the parent yells louder still and gets more severe to stop the child's reaction. Perhaps these are reasons why parental punishment is three times as high in families of severely aggressive children than in other families.

This may also explain why there are often conduct problems in children when parents go through a divorce or separation. It is *not* usually the parental separation that causes it; rather it is the marital conflict and disharmony leading up to the break between parents that does – the aggressive models they provide.

Families that do handle aggression effectively – that is, aggression does appear, but declines in frequency and is replaced by appropriate social and verbal skills – typically have many of the following characteristics:

- They give warnings before using punishment.
- They are careful not to take out other stresses and frustrations on the child (or other family members), so the child is not punished "for nothing" (when he has done nothing wrong).
- They prefer reason and explanation to punishment, reserving punishment for when this doesn't work.
- They are generous in the attention and praise they give to children for the good things they do.
- A child's aggression is never allowed to "work" – it does not get the child his way.
- They model or teach appropriate *alternatives to aggression* – requests, compromising, sharing, co-operation, turn-taking, helping others, etc.

These are the characteristics we will in fact try to practise (described below) in handling aggression in our own child.

When aggression is and is not a problem

If aggression should increase (especially after two years of age), remain a predominant way in which the child tries to get what he wants, then it is a problem. Usually this will be accompanied by other difficulties: the child has few, if any, friends and is in fact unpopular; there is a general problem of noncompliance; he shows little remorse, conscience, or sadness when he destroys property or hurts others; he seems to lack affection; he rarely co-operates, shares, or helps others; he is a "problem" at preschool; and he may fall behind in academics – language, colors, letters, numbers, etc. Severely aggressive children will show many of these associated problems. If your child does not, then his aggression is probably quite normal (though still unacceptable).

A simple little "test" that has often worked for me is to see how hard it is to get compliance. Most children with a serious problem of aggression are also very noncompliant. If your child is compliant to most (60-80 percent) requests, and a firm, strong, direct *demand* will ensure compliance when needed, then chances are that your child's aggression is not really serious (though it of course should still not be supported or permitted). Any parent concerned about aggression should also read the section on non-compliance (pages 118-127).

How to handle aggression
There are several positive, constructive ways we can react to aggression in order to both decrease it and teach appropriate alternatives.

1. *We make sure that aggression does not serve to get the child his way.* Most aggression in children is manipulative. A child may want something – a cookie, a toy, to play, to get on the swing (now), to go first. Or a child may do it to get out of something he does *not* like – putting on his jacket, cleaning up the toys, going to bed, taking medicine, etc. No matter what form the aggression takes the child must not get his way. Once aggression has started, you *cannot* give him that cookie; despite his aggression, we put on his jacket or carry him (kicking and screaming, if necessary) up to bed.

2. *We give warnings before we follow through or use punishment.* "If you don't head up to bed by the time I count to three, I will take you to bed and we won't read a story." This sort of warning is common, and will quickly become quite effective *if* you follow through . . . and you will have to a few times. The child should stop what he is doing, and *begin* to follow your directions before you hit "3" (it does *not* mean he has to be in bed, or have his jacket on and be in the car by the time you hit "3").

A second type of warning is to let the child know ahead of time that we'll have to go to the store "in five minutes." This is always a good idea, but is particularly helpful in those situations where you anticipate some difficulty (aggression). Instead of forcing a child to abruptly stop what he's doing, we give him a few minutes to finish up and prepare himself for a change in activities.

3. We are particularly careful to give our praise and attention when the child is behaving well – we look for things to praise. Under no circumstances do we let punitive interactions dominate our relationships with children. A general guideline is that there must be *at least five to six times as much praise* as reprimands, follow-through, warnings, or punishment. While this may seem obvious and natural, it really is not. We tend to jump when something is wrong, not when the child is quiet and well-behaved. It is the disruptive behavior that gets our attention naturally, not the good things that children do. Whenever we do impose controls on a child (reprimands, warnings, etc.) we must be particularly aware of opportunities to praise the child: because negative interactions are a bit more frequent during aggressive phases of development, positive and loving interactions must be increased also.

4. We make sure to teach the child appropriate ways to get what he wants (alternatives to aggression). We show him how to offer a toy in exchange for using another child's toy. We teach him that both children can play at the game, or take turns. We teach a child to ask nicely for what he wants. We teach him to co-operate, compromise, help, and comfort others – and we shower him with praise and affection when he does it. To teach a child these skills, we demonstrate, practise, explain the benefits of acting this way, and point out that heroes do this (using puppets is often very helpful). In addition, we try not to say "No." Rather, we try to say, "Yes, you can have that after Aaron is done (when mommy comes home, after dinner, on your birthday)", if he does ask nicely. In this way, he is successful, even if it is delayed, and this will be in stark contrast to the aggression, which never works (and often costs him his story, play, or TV-time).

5. Don't start a war unless you are sure you're going to win. If you're too tired or busy to deal with aggression, ask your spouse to do the bedtime routine, or else don't start it at all – let the child just fall asleep when he gets tired on the floor or sofa. Nothing could be worse than telling him it's time for bed, or he can't have that toy, and then giving in when he gets aggressive; this will teach him that if he perseveres, or gets more extreme, he will get his way. If you're in a public place (and you get embarrassed too easily – remember, every parent has gone through this), you should either let him have his way before he gets aggressive, or else you take him (kicking and screaming) out of the toy store or restaurant when he becomes aggressive. At times, it may seem like a "war" – the child will at first get more extreme in an attempt to get his way. But this will not last long, only until the child learns that aggression does not work. The more consistent and firm you are, the quicker he will learn it.

6. *There can be a cost attached to aggression.* There are several important points to remember about the use of reprimands, punishment, and the like. *First*, don't tackle ten things at once – if you're trying to handle aggression, don't start a new bedtime routine, toilet training, or anything else that can be upsetting. *Second*, we all have moods, other stresses, distractions, and so on. But we can't treat children negatively, unless it's for something *they* did. We can say, "I'm sorry, honey, but daddy has something else he has to do right now," rather than "No! Leave me alone." Negative reactions, when the child has done nothing wrong, will cause confusion, upsets, sadness, and depression, and of course will result in similarly negative actions by the child. If you reprimand a child, it should only be for something *the child* did wrong, and the reprimand should include a description or explanation of what he did wrong ("I'm not going to play with you because you hit me.").

Third, if we do use punishment of some sort, it must be effective (a real cost). It does no good to turn off the TV if he's not watching it, or to take away one toy if he's got 800 others. And verbal abuse, shaming, and nagging are all both inappropriate and ineffective. Alternatively, we can teach the child that aggression leads to bad things: by taking a child off the playground (i.e. let him just watch the other children play, or else take him home) if he pushes a child on the playground; taking away all his toys, or the one he is playing with, if he gets aggressive during play; giving a firm, sharp reprimand – abruptly grab both arms, bring him suddenly toward you, look him straight in the eye with a firm glare (with your faces only a few inches apart), and give a sharp, firm "NO HITTING."

Whether or not to use spanking is an ethical decision – one I cannot make for you (see discussion of "Punishment," pages 45-52); although it is often quite effective, it is not necessary in most cases, especially if aggression is not a frequent or pervasive style in your child. Moreover, it is something the child may copy if it lasts very long or occurs too often. It must be effective and work quickly if it is to be used at all.

A final note. If aggression is severe and frequent, or is associated with many other problems described earlier (dislike by peers, poor social skills, noncompliance, lack of remorse or feelings when another child is hurt, etc.), one should seek professional assistance to guide and supervise the handling of aggression. This does not mean the child has some deep inner psychic problem, it is simply to ensure that we do react to the aggression properly and effectively, that it is monitored, and that it begins to decline.

Counteraggression

A major issue for many parents is what to tell a child after he has been hit or pushed by another child. Should he fight back?

The first step here is to ensure that the other (aggressive) child is stopped. We cannot and should not allow our child to be hit, bitten, picked on, teased, pushed, or bullied on a regular basis. It could be very harmful to our child, as he may develop insecurities, fear or a dislike of school, embarrassment, isolation and fear of playmates, together with a poor self-image and little confidence. All children are pushed at times: for example, when another child wants to go first on the swing. This is not a major problem, it happens to all kids, and there is no real damage done. If, however, an aggressor picks on the *same* child(ren) regularly, then it *must* be stopped, one way or another.

There are several ways to stop another child's aggression. We can tell our child to hit him back; we can request that the teacher watch for it (or teach our child to tell the teacher), and have the teacher put a stop to it; we can go to the school or playground ourselves and reprimand the child for aggression; or we can speak to the parents of the aggressive child and ask for their help in controlling it.

While many people will argue about whether a child must learn to "fight his own battles," "take care of himself," and "fight back," this is much less important than first making sure that the aggression is stopped. Many children are quite sensitive and shy, finding it extremely difficult to confront another child or push him back. Moreover, he may push back, at a parent's urging, at which point the other child reacts even more severely, bopping him on the nose – resulting in a more extreme upset for our child, as well as feelings of in-competence and failure.

It can be much more damaging to force our child to fight back – if he is too shy, or simply not as big, strong or co-ordinated as the other child – because *we* play it up into a big deal and it be-comes a standard which the child may have a difficult time living up to. Moreover, if we nag, shame, punish, or constantly egg on the child, he may get downright neurotic about it – being obsessed with the bully or some pretty weird (negative) thoughts about himself, being fearful of school and playing with peers, avoiding the parent, lying to cover up, etc.

In such cases, either we must take care of the problem our-selves (by approaching the teacher, the child's parents, or deal-ing with the child directly), or else we can take our child to a self-defense course – which many children (even shy children) really like because it is relaxed, non-threatening, and (to the child) totally unrelated to the problem he is having with the bully. We can do both – put a stop to it ourselves for now, and try to prepare the child for any such future situations (teach him to tell the teacher or take him to a self-defense class, etc.).

For a child who is sufficiently assertive, the question of whether or not he should fight back (as opposed to walk away, tell the teacher, etc.) is an ethical decision that must be left to each parent. If the child is willing and able to "fight back" – that is, he does not have to be pushed or pressured into it – then it can help to teach something about self-reliance.

At the same time, if a parent does suggest this to a child, or give a child permission to fight back, it brings with it certain other parental responsibilities. We must also teach the child when to fight *and* when not to fight. Many children, once released from the controls on fighting, may begin to *start* fights in order to solve their problems, or they may react too excessively for the situation – hitting a boy in the face when that child just snatched his toy. In short, fighting can very easily get carried away, until it becomes a general strategy for dealing with any frustrations or disputes. A parent should restrict a child's fighting to "fighting back" ("First, let's tell Johnny it's your turn, not his. *If* he tries to hit you, or push you, *then* you can push him back, harder"), and make sure that the counteraggression is appropriate to the situation at hand.

Social behavior and relationships

Why is she so shy?"; "Why is he standing off by himself instead of playing with other children?"; "Geez, is he selfish – he's a spoiled brat, and won't share anything with anyone!"; "I'm really worried. He doesn't have any friends . . . doesn't seem to get along with anyone." Also, kids can seem so unfeeling at times – they may not feel like hugging us when we really want a hug, or they can say "mean" things that seem so unkind and unfair.

Most children at times become withdrawn, shy, lack affection, and they all have trouble sharing. This is rarely anything to worry about (until the grade-school years) because, as the child matures, she will naturally become more socially competent and able. In truth, the problem often lies in the parents' expectations – after a child learns to talk pretty well, he just seems like a "big boy" and we assume an awful lot; we forget that he's just learning the ropes, he's still just a child, exploring, testing, and self-centered.

Still, even knowing that your child will grow out of it, you may feel that the child is missing something, something you know he would like if he would only join in instead of sitting on the sideline. Even though it is not a serious problem, we can still help.

The only times when social immaturities turn into a real concern are: when they interfere with normal daily functioning – for example, the child who *never* plays with other children, but just sits and watches; when they last too long – if a six-year-old still refuses to share anything; or when they occur to excess – the child never shows affection to anyone. This will show up in many ways – a lack of friends, difficulties at preschool, playing alone instead of together with other children – and will be readily apparent as a "problem" to most parents.

Friendship

Friendships are crucial to a child. Nothing will facilitate social skills more than having a friend; few things will cause more personal anxiety and social problems than having no friends. It is important. It can be a pretty lonely place for adults if they have no friends, and it is no less true for children.

Fortunately, friendships are relatively easy to make for young children – after all, most children have the same goals in life: to play. The key is to find another child he will play *together* with – rather than each playing alone – and without fighting. Then, he will have a friend – as long as mommy or daddy take the time to invite the other child over, and visit their house, regularly.

The child needs a good friend, at least one. If there are concerns about isolation, sharing or affection, whether at school or at home, this friend will be an invaluable aide and "teacher." So we ask our child who his favorite children are at preschool, and then invite each one over (separately) until you see a friendship click. Then we invite that child back, take them to the movies together, let him spend the night. Since that child is in the same preschool class, they will do things together there, too, and your child will show substantial gains in participation, affection, sharing, and the like. Once into the swing of things, he will make more friends, too.

A parent should take an *active* role in helping here – we must find out from the teacher (or the child) which of the other children he likes; invite that child (and the parents, at least the first time) over; pick a child who is in the same preschool class so that the new relationship and social behaviors can carry over to that setting; invite only one child at a time (as groups of three tend to break down into a group of two and an outsider). This will be of *great* benefit to your child, especially if it is a new class or school, or you have moved to a new neighborhood, as it will ease the entry onto the playground or into the child's new pre-school.

Sharing

The three- to four-year-old is typically very possessive, and it would not cross his mind to simply give (lend) one of his favorite toys to another child – what for? If another child reaches for it, don't be surprised if your child bellows, "It's mine," clutches it, pouts, and goes to hide it in his secret hiding place. Even if he does not want to play with it, "It's (still) mine," and the intruder must be blocked from reaching the treasure at all costs. The child is still thinking about it, and worrying about it, even though the other child has long since moved on to other toys and forgotten about it.

There are several ways we can help that child to share. The place to start is to make sure we (a parent, sibling or friend) have something that the child wants. In order to get it from you, he has to offer something *of value* in return. You do not give him a new bicycle for a stick of bubble gum (then again, some kids do think it's a fair trade – they don't seem to count how long and hard you had to work to buy it). If your child offers diddly in return for a ride on a shiny new bike, say, "No, I don't want that; I want to use your (favorite) sword." Suggest one of his *favorite* toys. In this way, he is not only learning to share his toys with other children, but you are also teaching him appropriate "negotiation" and problem-solving skills to get what he wants, and these (if successful) can replace aggression, tantrums, crying, lying, grabbing, sneaking, stalking, and other covert intelligence operations to appropriate other people's things. We praise the dickens out of the child when he does share, and we point out the nice effects it has on other people – "Look how happy you made Cary. I think she likes you a lot – see, she's smiling. Aren't you proud of yourself that you made her so happy? What a big boy you are!"

A second place to help teach sharing is in the presence of younger or (physically) smaller children. For some reason, children are much more apt to share, co-operate, and help children smaller than themselves. I've seen many bullies let a meek, shy little girl play with the toy or the swing, yet kick the next guy who dares to take a turn. My own son refused for a while to give anything to anyone as big as him, but gave away the store to younger children (often before they even asked). We can easily arrange such opportunities.

In all such cases, we praise – lavishly – every instance of sharing (and all of these social skills). We tell the child, "Oh, I'm so-o-o proud of you for letting Nicole use your toy! You're such a wonderful boy! Gimme a hug, OK." The bear hug completed, with associated kissing and tickling, the child feels pretty good about the whole thing. The child will not only become interested in sharing, but he will learn that it is a magic word, a magic act, that it is expected and desirable – don't be surprised to see that child come running into the house saying, "I shared with John. I gave him my sword to use. Am I a big boy? Is mommy proud?"

I have seen so many parents try to "teach" sharing by demanding it ("Give that to your sister!"), and it just won't happen that way. The child "hooks" on (responds to) the parent, the demand, instead of learning the benefits, nuances, bartering, and compromising involved. It's not a preferred way to go, because it *just teaches compliance to demands, not sharing in a true sense.* The only time demands are called for is when the child is being unreasonable – for example, she simply won't give back another child's toy, in which case you demand that she give it back, taking it from her if necessary, and tell her (briefly) why she is being unreasonable and unfair.

Withdrawal, isolation, shyness

If a child stands off to the side watching other children play, rarely participating herself, we can help in several ways. But first, to know what to do, we must know *why* our child is not participating. There are several possibilities.

Some children don't participate because they don't know how; perhaps they don't know the game or the song. We should then teach it to our child (later, when no other children are present). We play the game or song with her (borrow the record, borrow a ball, go to the playground with her, etc.), and show her each step of the way. As she gets better, she will be more apt to play with her peers.

Some children don't play together with other children because they're too shy or afraid. We deal with it like any other fear – leading her to it in very small steps and relaxing, talking, and playing at each step along the way. I might go with her on the playground at first, hold her hand if necessary, and I'll play too – she's at the center of action with me. I then encourage her to "try just one kick," "just one throw," or "please help me throw it" (and we do it together). As she is kicking more and more, I may "accidentally" lose my grip on her hand because I had to jump over here to get the ball – I stay over here for a few minutes, wait to see if she'll continue to play, and roll her the ball if necessary to keep her involved. This might continue for five to ten minutes (or three days), and then I'll say, "Oops, got to get something; be back in a minute," at which point she is now playing on her own with the other children. One can use much smaller steps than this if necessary – for example, start a new game with just one other child (at home or at school), then build it up to two other children, etc.

A third reason children don't participate is that they get a lot of personal attention from adults when they are off by themselves. They stand out more, and it is natural for a teacher or parent to go talk to that child, stay with her, and do something else together. The child quickly learns that *not* participating leads to lots of personal attention. In such cases, the parent or teacher should provide that attention and affection *for playing*, not for standing off alone. "If you join in for a minute, I'll watch." When she touches the ball, touches or talks to another child, turns in a circle, or blinks, we say (excitedly), "Way to go Jenny! You're great! I didn't know you knew how to play the game!" We just want to praise her for being there, so at first we'll praise her no matter what she is doing. And the adult stays . . . providing attention and affection *for playing*, rather than for not playing.

Sometimes a child doesn't join in because he just doesn't like that game, or prefers doing something else more. This, of course, is nothing to worry about because the child is not really avoiding groups or play in a general sense and should not be considered withdrawn, isolated, or shy.

Helping others

There are two general strategies for encouraging a child to help others. First, we can subtly make the good things in life dependent upon two people getting something done together, or their getting it done faster. "OK, we can watch *Star Wars* if *you both* have your pajamas on by 7 o'clock. Benjamin (bigger brother), Rebecca doesn't know how to do some of it, so you can help her, OK?", or "We can't go outside until Johnny's toys are cleaned up; it's hard for him, Max, so if you help then we can all go out sooner." In this way, we can creatively "require" a child to help, without using demands, coercion, or nagging. The challenge is to think of ways in which helping must occur in order for something nice to follow for them both. It's not that hard, if we think about it – "Both of you must have your teeth brushed before we read a story"; "The dishes have to be put in the sink before anyone can play"; etc. Of course, we must keep an eye out so that one child doesn't take advantage of the situation. But that is easy to correct should it happen ("Let Gerry put the green blocks away – he has to do some, too.").

A second way to foster helping is to put a child in a situation where there is the opportunity, and the ability, to help another child. In such situations, children almost always help – perhaps just to show off what they know, but they do help. If your child is good at reading letters, play a letter game of some sort – for example, if the game stops until the other child answers, you will probably find that your child helps him. The same is true for sports, opening a box, naming the dinosaurs, etc. The key is to watch for those opportunities, even set them up, so your child's mastery permits him to easily help the other child. Then, of course, we praise "How helpful you were to Billy – that was wonderful." We don't praise how smart he is here because we don't want him to answer in place of or before Billy; we want him to *help Billy answer*. It is therefore crucial to wait until Billy answers, praise Billy, and then praise your child for helping Billy.

In addition, if a child has friends, you will see them already helping each other on occasion. If you want to increase how often your child helps others, then look for those times he already does, and praise him for it. This tells him that helping is a good thing, that it leads to good things, that his friend appreciates it and likes him more for it. When I roughhouse with my son and his friends, I often "trap" one child in my ultra-tickle-lock. It is amazing what happens when I say, "No one can save you now – ha ha ha": saviors come out of the woodwork. Other kids put their lives on the line, throw caution to the wind, in order to attack or tackle me and save the laughing lad in distress. The trapped child may call out, "Neil, help me," and Neil tries like the devil to do just that (and of course he does save him). What happens afterward is even more magical – they may thank each other; the saver hugs or puts an arm around the savee, and says "You awright?"; they help each other plan their next attack on the Tickle-Monster – all the time co-operating, sharing, showing affection, and helping with a growing, strengthening friendship.

Affection

The best way to facilitate affection is to model it, show what it's for and what effect it has on people, and then ask for it now and then.

If you pick up your child, give lots of hugs and kisses, hold hands, and let him sit in your lap with your arm around him while reading a story, he will want to do the same to imitate you. (He may actually put his arm over your shoulder while you're reading – sheesh.) Look first at how often you model it, how often you do it with your spouse, children, relatives, and friends because children who have a hard time displaying affection often have parents who also tend not to show their affections and feelings. Perhaps we just need to loosen up a bit. Some parents give a child a hug and kiss every morning when she wakes up, with a cheerful, "Good morning, it's going to be a fun day"; they may do the same at night when she goes to bed, and when the parent gets home from work. Of course, we do it at other times too, whenever it comes naturally, but you can rest assured she is getting lots of exposure to it if there are a few times each day where it is relatively "automatic" and expected (but never fake). In no time, children begin to initiate the same (affectionate) behavior; she'll come running into your bedroom to give you "your" hug and kiss in the morning.

What makes affection a bit easier to promote than other skills (reading, arithmetic) is that it naturally leads to nice things. When my son comes running toward me after I get home from work, I naturally lift him up to get that "good-huggin'" – and he loves being lifted up. Along with the bearhug, I may tickle him, tell him how big his muscles are getting, lift him on my shoulders, hold him out like an airplane and fly him around the room. Any child will be full of affection if it leads to wonderful, close contact and play – it often does happen quite naturally, and certainly should.

Caring about other children, as opposed to parents, is a slightly different matter; we have less control over what the other child does, how he reacts. The key here is not to force affection, but look for the right child to befriend. Don't expect affection and friendship to occur with all children (or adults) – they have their preferences, as you do. The key is to *sample* other children – invite them (individually) to the house – until your child obviously enjoys being with one of them. He will tell you. He will ask for the other child, or you can ask him, "Did you like playing with Larry today?" When it goes well, have the child come again in a few days, or go to his house. As the relationship progresses, so will caring and affection.

Someone once said that we "should not trifle with affections," and though he said it in another context, it applies here. Our task is to *find* a child's preferred object of affection, not to force affection (if such can ever be done) where it does not naturally belong.

A caveat: the cult of extroversion/the pathology of popularity

We must be careful not to succumb to the "Cult of Extroversion." Our society does strongly value the ability to initiate and maintain positive social relationships – people who are "outgoing," "active," and "gregarious" are deemed attractive and exciting.

Yet, to strive for popularity is to put all the rewards and pleasures of life in the control of others – it is an insecure, unhappy pursuit. It's a sad life, and I've seen too much of it, where people live and die for what others think. They have little time for anything else, never stopping to smell the flowers, and the grass is always greener somewhere else. We will all be popular at times, even wildy so, and we will be unpopular at times, – but both are fleeting, and impossible to maintain. What is important is to have some good friends. We should not . . . must not . . . teach our children to pursue popularity for its own sake.

There are no (known) optimal levels of peer interaction, friendships, sharing, or affection. Low levels of social involvement do not mean that there is a problem, or even that higher levels are desirable. A child who has no friends, and stands alone in all settings, does have a problem and we should help. A child who has "only" one or two friends, and plays only in some group activities, is probably fine – just very selective. In fact, some researchers claim that it is the gifted children who often prefer to do things on their own, although they can act in socially appropriate ways when necessary or when they are so inclined.

A distinction between *rejected* and *neglected* children is an important one. Studies have shown that "neglected" children – perhaps shy, quiet, often unnoticed or ignored by other children, sometimes preferring to do something else or to be on their own – grow up to live normal well-adjusted lives; on the other hand, "rejected" children – whom other children actually avoid, dislike, and refuse to play with – will often have severe adjustment problems in later life. It is only the rejected children that we need to worry about.

We must all question in ourselves what is really important and helpful to our child – we do not want them to be "rejected children," yet we must not concentrate so much on social skills that popularity becomes a primary pursuit for its own sake. The very, very large majority of our children are well within the normal range, and it is our tinkering with social skills that at times can push them to one extreme or the other – making them feel self-conscious, overly concerned about "doing something wrong," until they prefer to avoid social situations altogether, or they become unhappy unless they are (always) the center of attention.

Hyperactivity

During the last five to ten years, the topic of hyperactivity has emerged from relative obscurity to become one of the most frequently diagnosed and widely researched problems, and certainly one of the most common complaints among parents. Approximately half of all parents complain that their child is overactive ("constantly on the go", "bouncing off the walls") at one time or another. In the 1950s, hyperactivity was viewed primarily as a problem of middle childhood; however, it is now *defined* as a problem beginning before the age of seven. This serves of course to focus even more attention and concern on the activity level of young children.

The concern on the part of parents (and some professionals) has gone way overboard, unfortunately. What is meant by a professional diagnosis of hyperactivity is quite different from what the public generally means by the term – it is in fact much more than an "overactive" child. Much has been made of the problems that follow a hyperactive child – and these problems are real – but the very large majority of highly active ("overactive") children are in fact not hyperactive and have no problem whatsoever.

Let's begin with definitions of "hyperactivity" and a high activity level, so we can separate the problem behavior from the normal, developmental phases that children go through.

The highly active child
The highly active or overactive child does not present a real problem, though he may well test his mother's patience. Parents typically use the terms "hyperactive" or "overactive" simply to

describe concerns they have about the activity level of their child. Parents often use the term if their child has times when he is "constantly on the go," seems more active than other children, is sometimes "out of control," or "gets into everything."

A child is much more likely to be termed overactive by a parent if his *specific* activities (rather than the activity *level*, per se) require the frequent attention of the parent. For example, a child who gets into the medicine cabinet, electrical outlets, and "disappears" outdoors is much more likely to be called "overactive" than a child who is just as active but stays in the living room playing with friends or toys.

All of these behaviors are *extremely* common, however, particularly in boys. It is quite normal. In fact, such high activity levels, and extensive exploring, have been described as *characteristic* of the four-year-old, but may occur anytime, even in infancy (i.e. excessive squirming, wiggling, arm, leg, and head movements). Children simply go through periods when they are more or less active, explore and get into things, get excited or "wound up" and seem out of control. In the vast majority of children, it will pass or at least diminish very substantially by the time they are seven years old.

Definition of hyperactivity

Hyperactivity is much more than a highly active or very curious child who is "constantly on the go" or "gets into everything." A list of the specific criteria which define hyperactivity are presented in Table 4-5, and the more salient characteristics can be summarized as follows. *First*, hyperactivity means that the child has extensive difficulties in three areas: attention, impulsiveness, and high levels of inappropriate activity. *Second*, it means that a child has consistent and pervasive problems in these three areas. *Third*, it means that these difficulties worsen in structured situations and when self-control is called for – in preschools, during "quiet time" when you're trying to read a story, in waiting his turn during group play, in cleaning up the blocks he has been playing with, and so on. *Fourth*, all of this must last for at least six months before it would even be considered as possible hyperactivity.

Table 4-5
Definition of Hyperactivity (adapted from the *Diagnostic and Statistical Manual of Mental Disorders*, DSM-III)

In comparison to his or her age group, the child displays *excessive* signs of inappropriate attention, impulsivity, and high activity levels. These typically worsen in structured (i.e. classroom) situations, and at times when self-control is called for.

1. *Inattention.* Displays a majority of the following:
   a. usually fails to finish things he starts
   b. often doesn't listen or watch
   c. is easily distracted
   d. has difficulty on any tasks or activities requiring sustained attention
   e. has difficulty learning

2. *Impulsivity.* Displays a majority of the following:
   a. frequently acts without thinking
   b. shifts constantly from one activity to another
   c. has difficulty organizing play or work materials
   d. needs excessive amounts of supervision
   e. has difficulty awaiting turns during group play

3. *Activity Level:* Displays most of the following:
   a. runs about or climbs on things excessively
   b. has difficulty sitting still or fidgets excessively
   c. has difficulty staying seated
   d. moves about excessively during sleep
   e. is always "on the go" or acts as if "driven by a motor"

4. Onset before the age of seven

5. Duration of at least six months

Source: American Psychiatric Association, *Diagnostic and Statistical Manual* (DSM-III) Washington, D.C.: American Psychiatric Association, 1980.

The hyperactive child generally has difficulty *attending* to tasks or instructions – it may "go in one ear and out the other," or he may be easily distracted by every little noise and movement. The difficulty of *attending* is in fact so common in such children that hyperactivity has been called an "Attention-Deficit Disorder" by some. The term *"impulsivity"* implies poor self-control, excitability, an inability to wait or inhibit actions – the child may climb on rooftops or ledges (and even jump off), or jump into the swimming pool without knowing how to swim.

For the hyperactive child, a problem (excess) in *activity level* is particularly evident when structure or demands are placed on the child. Research has actually found no differences in activity level between normal and hyperactive children during unstructured or free-play time, but the hyperactive child has difficulty *controlling* his activity level, changing it, quieting, or calming down during structured times.

Children's overall level of activity may not be the critical element in identifying hyperactive children. Rather, whether or not their behavior is frequently disruptive, noncompliant, and "off-task" may be more important. A child who is unable to keep his hands to himself, is too loud, often doesn't listen to adults, or who runs off in different directions, may constantly come to the attention of a parent or teacher. A child who is just as active, but doing appropriate things (play), may be judged to be normally active. The former child may be thought of as hyperactive because of the conduct problems he presents, despite the fact he is no more active than the other child. In fact, there is some question as to whether hyperactivity is indeed different from a conduct problem – some researchers feel no difference exists.

Incidence of, and other problems associated with, hyperactivity

The peak age of referral (to a professional) for hyperactivity is eight to ten years of age. These are the early school years, when problems caused by hyperactivity become particularly evident – a child now must sit at a desk for an extended period, study or follow along in a book, stay at one activity and in one place for a while, and clean up after himself.

While true hyperactivity is rare, when it does occur it should be dealt with. Otherwise, studies have shown that hyperactive preschoolers often continue to be hyperactive in middle childhood, and it is no longer felt that hyperactivity disappears naturally in adolescence. In fact, studies confirm that hyperactive children do not fare well during the adolescent years – they typically do poorly at school, appear to lack some of the basic social skills needed to be accepted by peers, and are more often considered to be aggressive and annoying.

Why are children hyperactive?

While high levels of activity ("overactivity") seem to be a normal stage of development for most children, and of little concern, hyperactivity itself (high levels of inattention, impulsivity, activity, and often conduct problems) remains a bit of an enigma. While we don't know very much about what does cause hyperactivity, it will at least be comforting to know what does not cause hyperactivity.

Hyperactivity does not mean that there is any organic (brain) damage. One of the first theories of hyperactivity, which has unfortunately persisted in the public eye, is that it is associated with "minimal brain damage." Numerous studies, however, have failed to find any link between brain dysfunction and hyperactivity, and this assumption has now been effectively discredited. In fact, only about 10 percent of hyperactive children show any history of brain damage.

Diet and food additives have also received a great deal of publicity as causes of hyperactivity, particularly by parents and authors who value natural organic foods. While diet can play a role in hyperactivity, it generally does have an effect only with extreme deviations from a normal diet; the effects of diet are in fact much less dramatic than those claimed by parents and authors, and most hyperactive children do not show improvement when the diet is changed. Moreover, the usefulness of dietary changes, which are often difficult to put into practice and maintain, is highly doubtful when compared to the greater effectiveness of clinical interventions.

Some studies have reported that hyperactive children have

higher levels of lead in their bloodstream, and lead is known to cause irritability, short attention span, and learning difficulties. A common source of lead in the past has been lead-based paint, which children may chew, lick, or swallow. Such paints are no longer used, but are not uncommon in older buildings. Lead intake is now much more likely from industrial pollution and the use of leaded gasoline in automobiles. Still, the level of lead in hyperactive children was not found to be at toxic or dangerous levels, so most researchers feel that lead is at most a contributing factor, not a cause, of hyperactivity.

When "overactivity" is and is not a problem

A high activity level, by itself, is not usually a problem in children up to six years of age. Many children, especially boys, go through periods when they seem to be constantly on the go, even uncontrollable, during the course of normal child development. It is only when such activity levels are also associated with most of the excesses listed in Table 4-5, and this has persisted for at least six months, that hyperactivity would be considered. This is rare. The vast majority of parental concerns about activity level in their children are based upon the parents' lack of information about normal stages of development and appropriate levels of (over)activity.

What to do about high activity levels and hyperactivity

Even though high activity levels are common, and children typically grow out of them, a child who is constantly on the go can tax any parent's patience. There are things that can help during these times. In particular, encouraging him to sit on the sofa (quietly), *helping* him to clean up his blocks, *showing* him how to read the words in the book, using lots of praise for completing a task, as well as sitting quietly and attending, can have a very powerful effect on the highly active child. Some have added rewards, such as privileges (a favorite TV program, play time, going swimming, etc.), surprises (little things, from bubble gum to crayons) when the child does well, and even some reprimands (i.e. "Don't throw your toys around!") when the child behaves inappropriately.

In general, we keep a sharp eye out for when the child is over-doing it, and teach him that good things happen when he shows some self-control ("slows down"). We can say, "You can play with the racing cars after you put all the blocks away." Then, we hold the racing cars until it is done, and praise the child warmly when the task is accomplished. If he has trouble, we help him, show him – I may do the yellow blocks if he puts away the green ones; I may take turns with him, putting away one block if he puts away another. Similarly, when reading a story, we make sure to spice it up with adventure, action, sounds and noises, faces, and enthusiasm so it is *enjoyable* for him to attend. If he fidgets too much, jumps around, talks too loud or too fast, then we stop the story and tell him, "I can't read while you're doing that," and continue only when he stops. If he doesn't stop, we can say, "If you don't let me go on with the story, then I'm going to leave." If enjoyable things happen when he shows some con-trol, and unpleasant things happen when he is out of control, most children will control themselves, slow down, watch, and listen.

In handling a *hyperactive* child, I would not hesitate to get some professional assistance – the guidance and comfort will be very helpful and reassuring. I would look for someone with ex-tensive experience in this area, and someone who is not afraid to use rewards and consequences.

Other treatment alternatives which exist, like psychotherapy and dietary changes, have not proved to be effective in dealing with hyperactivity. Educational approaches, which stress quiet and non-distracting classrooms and cubicles, have not signifi-cantly improved the attention or academic achievement of hy-peractive children. Such approaches remain popular in some circles, but research has not found them to be effective.

Another very common approach to hyperactivity is the use of medication. This is unfortunate for many reasons, and usually is ineffective – I would recommend that parents stay away from therapists, family doctors, or psychiatrists who suggest medication right off the bat. In the long run, it appears that hyperactive children who receive medication are not better off than children who receive no medication. While drugs may in the short run "slow down" a child, they don't *teach* him anything. Unless teaching procedures are used, to establish task-completion, study skills, and/or attentional skills, drugs will only make the child less "trouble" for teachers or parents, but they will not help the child. Drugs alone appear to have little impact on the long-term social, academic, or psychological adjustment of the hyperactive child.

Obsessions, compulsions, and rituals

"Larry is absolutely obsessed with He-Man toys. He watches them on TV, wants to buy every new He-Man character they make, takes those characters with him everywhere – to the toilet, to school, to a friend's house, to the market, and to sleep. He has to wear his He-Man T-shirt, sleep in He-Man sheets (covered of course by a He-Man blanket), and get dressed in He-Man underwear, socks, pants, and shirts. He puts on a He-Man costume (mask, belt, chestplate, sword, boots) over the He-Man clothes so that he looks like the eight-foot He-Man poster on his wall, and then of course he wants to play He-Man all day. I'm so sick of that (bleep, bleep) He-Man – who says he's a good guy?"

This is just one of a zillion examples of "obsessions" children may have. At times, they can in fact drive a parent batty. It is, however, nothing to worry about; in fact, it is not an obsession.

Children lavish their time and attention on favorite things, activities, and people. Over time, the objects of their affection change – they grow out of He-Man, make new friends, discover new games (i.e. bike-riding, soccer) that will compete with the old ones (tag, hide-and-seek). The exclusivity of, or preoccupation with, certain toys, objects, activities, or people will simply diminish in most children as they get older, as they "discover" new ones that are as much or more fun.

Children under the age of six very rarely have an obsession; their preoccupation serves only to have fun, and have more fun with favorite toys, fantasies, and people. A real obsession is in fact serious, but it is much more than a preoccupation with toys, so it is important to know the difference between a preference or preoccupation on the one hand, and an obsession or compulsion on the other.

Definitions

An obsession, which would need to be treated, refers to persistent, repetitive, *anxious thoughts*; compulsions refer to persistent, repetitive, *anxious behavior*. They both focus on anxiety. For example, a child may wash his hands ten times per day because he is afraid of dirt; he may think about dirt, talk about dirt, refuse to go into other people's houses (they're too dirty), or refuse to play on the playground (it's too dirty) – he generally sees dirt everywhere. Dirt causes a tremendous amount of anxiety, and hand-washing rituals may develop to relieve that anxiety (get the dreaded dirt off). If this persists for a period of time (i.e. six months), and clearly interferes with normal daily activities (or is very bizarre and stigmatizing), then treatment would be considered.

This is very, very rare in children under six years of age. Most children become preoccupied with things: they have to have their security blanket; they won't step on cracks in the sidewalk; they want to hear certain songs or stories or watch certain shows, over and over and over again; they may demand to get dressed in a very particular way (zipping up the pants only after everything else is on), or stick rigidly to a specific order and sequence in the bedtime routine – teeth-brushing, toileting, putting the pajamas on, getting a drink, having a story, placing dolls in their "proper" place on the bed – and God forbid you should forget something during the bedtime routine because he may take off his pajamas, put all his clothes back on, put away the security blanket, in order to start it all over again and do it in the correct order.

Such routines, or a preoccupation with certain toys and heroes, are nothing to worry about. They have nothing to do with fear; it is not disruptive to daily functioning; it is not socially bizarre or stigmatizing. And the child will grow out of it without any special intervention.

If you should find that there is a great deal of anxiety in- volved, that it does interfere with important daily activities, and that it persists for at least six months, then it should be treated very much like a phobia (see discussion of "Fears and Phobias", pages 102-112). But this is so rare in young children that I would recommend that you get a second opinion from a psychologist before doing anything.

Epilogue: getting help

It's OK to get help

Parents should not be the least bit shy to seek help for their child. Unfortunately, some feel it is stigmatizing to the child (or family), that they should "work out their own problems," or that a therapist is only there for "deep" or "serious" problems. Not true.

First, you should know that virtually all licensed therapists are required to maintain confidentiality. They cannot disclose anything about you or your child — even your name — to anyone without your permission. There are few exceptions to this (i.e. in the case of child-abuse, or if the child is a danger to himself or others), and parents can rely on the fact that what is said between them and the therapist remains confidential.

In the big picture, parents must realize that what is good for the child is more important that whether you solved the problem yourself, whether it was "serious" or not. If the child progresses, then everyone will feel happier; parents will feel better about themselves and the child. Thoughts of whether it was serious or not, whether you "needed" a therapist, will be soon forgotten if the child benefits.

A therapist is there to help you. If you have some concerns about your child, a therapist can at least provide some assurance as to whether the child will in fact grow out of it, or may provide guidance in helping your child to progress. The key, of course, is to find the right therapist.

To find the right therapist, parents can call the relevant licensing boards or associations (i.e. for psychology, speech therapy, etc.) which are listed in the phone book, ask the family physician, friends, or call the relevant department at a university or hospital. It is important to keep in mind, however, that these are just "leads" — it will be up to you to decide which therapist is best (see below for some suggestions and questions to ask).

When to get help

In this book I have tried to clarify when different kinds of child behavior are a problem, and what the literature suggests we can do about it. The programs I have described, however, are not tailored to your specific child; they are examples, principles, from my experience and the literature. You will need to tailor that program for your child, and if you need help in doing so a therapist should be consulted.

If the behavior simply concerns you a lot, then it can help to consult with someone who knows more about it. Chances are there is nothing to worry about, and you will be happy to know that. If some intervention is suggested, however, you can be pleased that you caught it early and gave your child the best chance for success.

The bottom line is whether or not the child improves. If despite your best efforts the child is not improving, then you should definitely seek some help.

Characteristics of a good professional/program

There are several characteristics that I would look for in finding the right professional/program for my child:

1. I want a program that tailors the treatment to my child, rather than one that has a set program they give to every child.

2. I want a therapist who uses the principles described in this book (Part 3). While they may add, change, or otherwise alter these, I want to hear them talk about praise,

feedback, modelling, etc., for these principles are embedded in much of the literature that has proven to be helpful in changing and improving children's behavior.

3. I want a therapist who focuses on the behavior of concern, not on deep inner psychic conflicts of my child.

4. I want a therapist who expects improvement in a relatively short time (i.e. three to six months), not one who expects treatment to last "indefinitely" or for years.

5. I want a therapist who designs a specific program, and teaches me how to help, not one who simply talks to or plays with my child for an hour each time.

6. I want a therapist who is willing to go where the problem is — to the preschool, my home, the playground if necessary — so that the treatment can be properly supervised and carried out in the environment in which the problem behavior occurs.

7. I want a therapist who knows more than I, who knows more than what is in this book, about the behavior (fears, speech, aggression, etc.) I am concerned about. I will discuss what I know (from the relevant sections of Part 4) and expect the therapist to know much of it, add to it, and to give me more information about the problem.

8. I want a therapist who focuses specifically on children, and who is experienced in handling the specific behavior I am concerned about.

9. I want a therapist who keeps up with the latest research and treatment techniques. If his bookshelf is covered with dust, there are no journals or books that go beyond 1975, and no certificates of continuing education hanging on his wall, I would leave.

10. I want a therapist who takes the time to explain things to me, who gets along well with my child, and who is not constantly watching the clock.

11. I want a therapist who talks about treatment, not just assessment; who spends a minimum of time assessing my child and most of the time planning, supervising, monitoring, or carrying out the actual treatment program.

12. I would want a therapist who has a license, a degree, a certificate to practise, and I would call the relevant licensing board or association (i.e. for psychology, speech therapy, etc.) to find out what kind of training is required to get that certificate. Advanced degrees (i.e. a Ph.D or a Master's degree) usually suggest that a person has met some standards for practising. On the other hand, in many places anyone can hang out a shingle saying he is a "behavior therapist," "child therapist," "family counsellor," etc. A group can get together, set minimal standards, and hand out "certificates" (some are even obtained through mail-order courses). This does not mean that they aren't good, it means that you must check more closely to find out what kind of skills, training, and experience they have.

What is an "assessment"? "diagnosis"? "prognosis"?

An *assessment* refers to the methods used for finding out what the problem is. There are an infinite number of ways to assess the neurological, cognitive, and behavioral functioning of a child. Most therapists do conduct interviews with the parents and observations of the child; some also use standardized tests for mental, social, or language development; others may use questionnaires or achievement tests; some may suggest a physical screening for genetics, vision, hearing, or other physical problems. Each of these tests give a result of some kind, and the results are taken together, evaluated, and used to come up with a *diagnosis*. The *diagnosis* is simply a label for the problem —

such as "hyperactivity," a "learning disability," or a "phobia" — which gives some focus to the treatment.

The *prognosis* simply means, "What are the future expectations for this child's behavior?" Will it probably improve? Worsen? Stay the same? Often, we can talk about two kinds of prognosis — *with* or *without* treatment. A good prognosis *without* treatment suggests that the child will probably grow out of it without any special intervention; a poor prognosis without treatment suggests that the child may not improve or may deteriorate if a treatment is not found. A good prognosis *with* treatment suggests that the child will probably improve *if* we carry out a specific program to help the child; a poor prognosis with treatment suggests that the child may not improve substantially even with the treatment.

Are assessment and diagnosis important?

Yes, they are, but we should not spend all our time assessing and labelling children. It is of course crucial to know what the problem is, and that's what the assessment can tell us. Often, however, the problem is obvious, and the assessment can be a simple matter; in most cases, there is no need for a battery of tests to measure everything under the sun. Some professionals do nothing but assessment, and they do a very thorough job of it — if you're not sure what the problem is, then such extensive screening may be called for. Most of the time, however, it won't be necessary.

Some parents (and professionals) are very concerned about labelling the behavior, looking at all its possible causes, and understanding how and why it happened. For most of us, however, it is more important to deal with the behavior, change it, and help the child. While assessment and diagnosis certainly have a place, their primary use is to help us decide what the treatment should be. Once we know that, further assessment of the child is usually not necessary (except of course in evaluating the effects of the treatment itself).

INDEX

About the Author

D r. Arnold Rincover is a licensed psychologist, Associate Professor at O.I.S.E. and the University of Toronto, and writes a weekly newspaper column on psychology for the *Toronto Star*. He has also been a Consultant to the Department of Psychology at the Hospital for Sick Children, and the Founding Director of the Experimental Preschool Project at the Surrey Place Centre. An internationally renowned researcher, speaker and consultant, Dr. Rincover is the author of academic textbooks and over fifty research publications on children's behavior. Born in Canada, Dr. Rincover currently lives in Toronto.